THE OLD TESTAMENT
IN DIALOGUE WITH MODERN MAN

THE OLD TESTAMENT IN DIALOGUE WITH MODERN MAN

by
James D. Smart

THE WESTMINSTER PRESS

Philadelphia

COPYRIGHT © MCMLXIV W. L. JENKINS

Scripture quotations from the Revised Standard Version of the Bible are copyright, 1946 and 1952, by the Division of Christian Education of the National Council of Churches, and are used by permission.

LIBRARY OF CONGRESS CATALOG CARD No. 64–14086

Jan., 1965

PUBLISHED BY THE WESTMINSTER PRESS ®
PHILADELPHIA, PENNSYLVANIA 19107

PRINTED IN THE UNITED STATES OF AMERICA

CONTENTS

PREFACE

THE EIGHT CHAPTERS of this book were delivered as the Carnahan Lectures at Union Theological Seminary, Buenos Aires, in Argentina in July, 1963. When I received the invitation to give the lectures, I had just published a book on Biblical hermeneutics, *The Interpretation of Scripture,* which by its nature was limited to a discussion of principles. I decided therefore to use this opportunity to develop a series of Old Testament expositions that would serve to illustrate the method of approach advocated in the former book. An introductory chapter could hardly be expected to condense the arguments that earlier had extended to some three hundred pages, but instead had to be focused upon the heart of the matter, the dialogue character of revelation, and the implications of this for an interpretation in which God is to speak his message afresh through Scripture into the life of our day. Consideration also had to be given to the fact that the lectures were to be addressed in translation to Spanish-speaking pastors in South America, many of whom would not be familiar with the literature of the debate on hermeneutics. Thus it was not in place to load the lectures with references to this literature or to introduce discussions that would assume a knowledge of it. English-speaking readers will find these references and discussions in *The Interpretation of Scripture.* For that reason, and since the book is most likely to be read by ministers, church school teachers, and laymen, it seemed wisest to retain the original, rather simple form of the lectures.

A very real factor in the choice of subject was the knowledge that in the younger churches in general a very acute situation exists in respect to the Old Testament. Either it is abandoned entirely in preaching or it is interpreted with such literalness that it becomes misleading to the church. Both alternatives silence the real message of the Old Testament with almost equal effectiveness. Why Christians, and especially Christian ministers, should think these are the only alternatives is hard to understand. But perhaps it is because the growing body of writings on the Bible that combine critical honesty with an awareness of the mystery of divine revelation in it have not yet begun to open up to them, and perhaps those writings fail to reach them because they remain so often on the level of general theological discussion and do not provide sufficient concrete illustrations of what should happen in the interpretation of specific passages of Scripture.

When one hunts through volumes of American sermons for instances of preaching on Old Testament texts, one becomes aware that an acute situation in this area exists also in our North American churches. More than one volume of sermons that have been heralded as a brave attempt to let the Old Testament speak have proved, on close examination, to reveal very little of the Biblical author's mind and a much larger measure of the preacher's mind on subjects only remotely connected with the Scripture under consideration. The disturbing reality is that even highly competent men who *want* to preach from the Old Testament frequently find themselves half-paralyzed when they attempt to do so.

Some years ago during a conference of ministers I was asked to meet at luncheon with five men who were between three and five years out of seminary. They were all deeply in earnest about the problems of their ministry, but at one point they found themselves at a loss. Their three years in seminary had convinced them of the necessity of the historico-critical approach to Scripture. There could be no return for them to any naïve literalism. But they had so little training in exegesis and exposition in seminary that they had no confidence in their ability to do for their people what their seminary professors had done for them. Their dealing with Scripture had remained too much on the level of general introduction to the problems, the literature, the history, and the theological ideas, and had not focused sufficiently upon the text of Scripture itself. Perhaps my answer to those five men at their luncheon table may be supplemented by these lectures and may take them and others a few steps down the road which they must learn to walk with confidence, each in his own place.

The title is too pretentious by far. It is not the whole Old Testament that is here in dialogue with modern man, but only seven brief passages from it. More could have been added indefinitely and it would still have been only a fragment of this vast treasure-house that we call the Old Testament. The only justification for the title is that in a real sense it is the whole Old Testament that speaks wherever its word is heard. Its words are one insofar as they are the medium whereby God speaks and in speaking comes to man. And when once a man has heard this word it is like a fire in his bones that refuses to be quenched, provoking him to listen again and again for what this strange and troubling book out of an ancient world has to say to him.

The first three lectures were given not only in Buenos Aires but also at Berkeley Baptist Divinity School in Berkeley, California, and as the Jackson Lectures at the Perkins School of Theology in Dallas, Texas. I would express my gratitude for the hospitality shown me in all three schools and especially for the delightful eight days which the faculty of Union Theological Seminary in Buenos Aires provided for myself and my wife.

J. D. S.

Union Theological Seminary
New York

I

THE RESTORATION OF DIALOGUE
IN BIBLICAL INTERPRETATION

DIALOGUE is a two-way conversation. Normally it takes place between two or more persons or between two groups of persons through their representatives. Therefore the idea of a dialogue between a modern man and a book that comes out of a world more than two thousand years removed from ours may seem strange, or even impossible, to some minds. It is not just that there are difficulties in the way of conversing with a book, any book, but particularly with one whose authors died so long ago. How does one ask them questions and get answers from them? But added to this is the fact that most people are accustomed to letting the Bible conduct a monologue. They listen respectfully, with a passive rather than an active mind, when they hear it read. When they read it themselves, it does not occur to them to ask it any very serious questions or to press it for answers. The Bible speaks and they listen. But the question is: Do they hear what is being said if they are not stirred to respond, to answer back, to question, to demand that they be told more? The verb " hear " in Hebrew significantly denotes not any passive receiving of words into the mind but the response of a man's whole being. The hearing of God's word is itself an act of obedience.

The sheer passivity which is so widely assumed to be an expression of respect for the Bible is exposed as hypocrisy as soon as a man comes into firsthand encounter with the word to which the Biblical records bear witness. The word of God is God in his word addressing man, and in addressing him, coming to him, offering himself and his gifts to him, claiming him in love for fellowship with himself, making him know his blindness and at the same time giving him sight. In this encounter no man can remain passive or silent. The approach of God in his word must be to him either a threat to his present existence, shaking him to the depths and rousing all his defensiveness, or the appearance of a liberator with the promise of a new life and a new world. Silent, passive respect means simply that this word has not yet been heard and this God who speaks in Scripture has not yet been encountered.

The thesis of these chapters is that this dialogue character is intrinsic to the content of Scripture and for that reason is essential to the interpretation of it. In the New Testament it is not difficult to show that at its center is the mystery of the communion of the Father and the Son, the Father making himself known in all the fullness of his grace and truth to the Son, and the Son living out his life among men as the moment-by-moment free response of his being to the Father. God's revelation in Jesus Christ is thus, from the beginning, a dialogue, and as Jesus draws men into dialogue with himself they are drawn into his own dialogue with the Father. His communion with the Father is reflected in his relationship with men, and in turn his relationship with men is reflected in *their* relationships with others. The dialogue reaches out in ever-widening circles, yet continually retains its center. Whether it is Jesus conversing with Simon the Pharisee, or Peter addressing a Jerusalem crowd, or Paul writing to the Corinthian church, we find ourselves somehow listening in on the same essential conversation, a conversation of God with man and of man with God in which man's very life is at stake. And, listening, we are suddenly drawn in to find that we are not outsiders but insiders and participants. Interpretation of the New Testament is therefore an extension of the circles of its dialogue to take in each new age.

It is equally true that the Old Testament has this dialogue character. It is misconceived when its content is taken to be a complex of religious ideas and practices or a body of divine truth that can be reduced to propositional form. The Old Testament is the record of a gigantic dialogue between God and Israel through more than a thousand years during which it was of the highest importance to preserve not just God's precious words to Israel but also an account of Israel's response to God. Revelation and response belong together and are inseparable because it is never an abstract truth about God or man that is revealed but rather, God himself in relation with man and man in relation with God. But in this dialogue with God, Israel is not an isolated fragment of humanity but is the representative of humanity. The covenant relation with God within which alone there is the promise of life for Israel reveals the hidden relation on which the life of all mankind depends. It is not just Israel but man as man who must live moment by moment by every word that proceeds out of the mouth of God, that is, by hearing and responding to God in personal relation. The Old Testament dialogue is a torso, an unfinished conversation in which the participants strain forward toward a revelation and response that are yet to come. Again and again in the Old Testament we as Christians are aware that there is a word that God has not yet spoken to man and a response that man, even the most consecrated man, has not yet been able to give to God. And yet we are made aware also that the story of Israel is our story and that the pilgrimage of Israel is our pilgrimage, so that unless we enter into Israel's dialogue with God we are unlikely to have ears to hear what is being said at the decisive climax of that dialogue in the New Testament.

In the light of these facts it is a reasonable conclusion that an interpretation of Scripture that intends to let the message of Scripture be heard in its integrity today must take account of this unique character of the content of Scripture. The basic problem with which it is confronted is how a dialogue between God and man that took place and is recorded in the language and thought forms of ancient eras in Palestine can actually be heard, understood, and entered into by modern man. There are those who think the difference in language and thought forms between then and now to be so great that it forms an insuperable barrier to the modern age. No one can deny that it constitutes a very serious problem which has to be faced courageously. But perhaps the present tendency is to exaggerate the difficulty and to ignore the fact that Israel itself, in Old and New Testament times, passed through a number of changes in language and thought forms without any break occurring in the continuity of the dialogue. The *form* of the dialogue changes and takes on new aspects, but in *substance* it remains the same dialogue. Of major significance is the fact that the human participants never feel bound by the forms that the dialogue has taken in the past, but are free, in fact are compelled by the integrity that their relation with God demands of them to be free to speak as men of their own time and place and culture. Apply this to our own modern situation and perhaps we have the key to interpretation. Our dialogue with God belongs to the twentieth century and has to take place in the language of our time and in relation to the realities of our time. Yet it is continuous with the dialogue of the Old and New Testaments, and our ears and our lips are opened to participation in it only as we recognize in the Scriptures our own immediate dialogue with God.

Our particular concern in these pages is to be with the Old Testament, attempting to see what happens when this conception of interpretation is applied to a series of Old Testament passages. There is reason to believe that the Old Testament has ceased to have any living voice in many quarters in the church. Godfrey Phillips (*The Old Testament in the World Church;* Lutterworth Press, London, 1942) some years ago warned us that the Old Testament had been almost totally abandoned in the younger churches. But the situation is equally serious in the older churches. One has only to think of what happened in Germany thirty years ago. Also, in the United States not only is the Old Testament conspicuously absent from the preaching of the churches but there are large denominations that have come to regard only the New Testament as basic to the Christian faith. We must note also that there are significant voices among the theologians of our day that insist that the Old Testament should no longer be regarded as Christian Scripture. The dialogue between the Old Testament and modern man has become a feeble thing. We are to ask now whether it is possible that this breakdown in the relation between the church and the Old Testament has been due to the failure of interpreters to recognize on the one hand the dialogue character of the Old Testament and on the other hand the necessity for our relation to the Old Testament in interpretation to be one of continuing dialogue.

Two methods of interpreting the Old Testament have shaped the preaching and teaching of the church for the past century, and frequently it has been assumed that they are our only alternatives. One hundred years ago English-speaking Protestantism was almost everywhere dominated by a literalistic view of Scripture that insisted upon the identity of every part of Scripture with the word of God and regarded the text as sacrosanct. The work of critical scholars who analyzed the various books, finding in them documents belonging to different ages and attempting to put every passage in its original historical situation, seemed nothing less than blasphemy, and eminent scholars were expelled from the church and from their teaching positions for adopting such views. Today the situation is reversed. Protestantism is dominated by the historico-critical view of Scripture, and in the leading seminaries a scholar who was shown to be a literalist in his approach to Scripture would be unlikely ever to be appointed to a professorship. But in the churches at large, literalism has managed to maintain its hold more tenaciously than in the seminaries, and a very considerable percentage of the men and women who volunteer for the ministry come from churches where they have known no other interpretation.

Literalism and literalists have survived in the churches not because of their repudiation of historical scholarship but in spite of it. They have survived because in an age when religion and morals rather than revelation became the primary interest of the church and of theology, when in fact it was no longer respectable to speak of a unique revelation of God in Scripture, they continued to insist that the Bible was God's word to man and that the Old Testament should be heard together with the New. They may sometimes have threatened to Judaize Christianity by their application of literalism to the Old Testament, and in their desire to defend the Bible they may have built a wall around it which to them was a wall of defense but which actually was a barrier obstructing the conversation between the Bible and modern man. Their most serious error, however, was in equating the text of Scripture with the word of God, pronouncing it to be an inerrant record of divine truth whose holiness forbade the mind of man to investigate it with unhampered freedom. This absolutizing of the text of Scripture concealed the dialogue character of revelation within the Scriptures and made it impossible for interpretation to take the form of an honest dialogue. The literalist stands accused therefore of not letting himself and his interpretation be ruled sufficiently by the character of the Scriptures themselves. They do not present him with a body of historical information, doctrines, truths, and principles to be accepted by him unquestioningly. They ask of him no sacrifice of intellect. On the contrary, they invite him with all his heart and mind to enter into the dialogue between God and man to which they bear witness, to hear and give answer honestly.

At the opposite pole from the literalist is the historical scholar. For two hundred years now he has labored untiringly to light up the dark places of Scripture by putting each passage, as far as possible, in its original historical setting. A vast range of linguistic, literary, historical, and archaeological resources have been brought to bear upon the text. One has only to compare a recent history of Israel or a commentary on any Old Testament book with a similar work of one hundred years ago to recognize the dimensions of the achievement. But frequently the assumption has been that, when once the history behind the text has been reconstructed and the text can be read in its original situation, it is a comparatively simple matter to extract from it the timeless truth that is relevant to our own age, leaving behind the more primitive features or elements that belong to the Biblical period alone. The historian also provides us with an orderly account of what the Hebrews thought about God, man, and the world at various periods in their history, and this is taken to represent the contents of the Old Testament in a form that we can assimilate today. But revelation, an actual dialogue between God and man, is an embarrassment to the historian. His methodology is equipped only to take the measure of human events, ideas, and practices. He cannot compass a history in which God's action precedes man's action and man's word is a response to God's word, so he tends to give us a history in which only man ever thinks, speaks, or acts, and the Bible becomes the book about man's thoughts concerning God and man rather than the recital of the mighty acts of God.

The very real contribution of the historian has been to search out for us in the minutest detail the human story of the Scriptures and to demonstrate for us how thoroughly human it really is. But he has been even more influential than the literalist, because of his intellectual prestige and growing authority, in concealing the dialogue character of Scripture. In his hands the Bible has become the record of a threefold religious development in Israel, Judaism, and Christianity rather than witness to a continuous dialogue between God and man, and its content has been assumed to be religious and moral truth that can be extracted from the ancient records and applied to life today in a purely rational operation rather than an actual encounter of God with man, the meaning of which in the ancient situation cannot begin to be grasped by the modern interpreter until he ceases to be a lordly spectator and lets himself as a modern man be drawn into the encounter.

The Existentialist Approach

Before we go any farther, we must consider the suggestion that is being made in some quarters that the Scriptures have become a closed book to modern man primarily because of the mythological character of so many of their statements. The modern world has abandoned the mythologies of a prescientific age, and a faith that continues to make use of a mythological framework in its expression is said to be simply incredible. Unfortunately there are several quite different issues mingled together in the work of Rudolf Bultmann, whose name is most closely associated with this problem. On the one hand he was one of the first scholars to rebel against the assumption of historical interpreters that they could extract a content of truth from the Biblical text in a purely objective fashion and to recognize that the interpreter must know himself to be involved in the text if it is to speak to him. He also led the way in insisting that the content of the text is a revelation of God in which God comes to man to redeem him. His great concern was that modern man might really be brought into the decision of faith by hearing this kerygmatic word of God, and to him the great obstacle in the way of such hearing was to be located in the mythological thought forms of the Biblical authors. His aim was not, like nineteenth-century liberals, to sweep away all that was mythological in utter disregard of what the Biblical witness was seeking to say in such terms, but rather, to translate the content of such mythological statements into terms comprehensible in the modern age. Thus far, we can only be grateful to him for laying open the dimensions of the problem. We cannot proceed to interpret Scripture as though the people to whom we are speaking live in a three-story universe or believe that their sicknesses are caused by demon possession or expect God to appear visibly or to speak audibly to them.

On the other hand, Rudolf Bultmann has complicated the dialogue with the Biblical authors by a number of assumptions concerning modern man that he has taken over from existentialist philosophy. Heidegger's definition of man as poised between inauthentic and authentic being seems to him to be a secularized form of the Biblical understanding of man and therefore an assumption that facilitates our dialogue with Scripture. But from the same source he draws the conviction that all statements concerning God must be reduced to the form of statements concerning man's self-understanding. This latter results in a vast extension of what is to be regarded as mythological: not just the three-story universe and demons and movements of supernatural beings in space, but literally all statements in Scripture about the supernatural. These are to be translated into statements by man about his own existence. Where this complicated process leads us may be very difficult to trace in detail, but some of the consequences have already been made very clear in Bultmann's writings. For the Old Testament the result is disastrous. The faith in God as Creator of heaven and earth and Lord of history with which the Old Testament is saturated becomes completely untenable. This is an ancient Hebrew mythology in which assertions are being made concerning God's relation to the world, and these assertions cannot be translated into terms of self-understanding. The most that can be asserted by any man is that God is his personal creator. What happens to the incarnation and the Holy Spirit in the New Testament is equally illuminating. The statement that God became man is mythological, since God must remain God, and man, man. For God to become man is impossible. The most that such a statement can mean is that Jesus was the bearer of God's word to man. Similarly, an indwelling of man by the Holy Spirit is impossible, since the autonomy of man is such that his existence cannot be penetrated by a supernatural spirit, either the spirit of a demon or the Spirit of God.

It begins to be clear that the existentialist approach to the dialogue with Scripture lays certain limitations upon it from the side of modern man. If the literalist was inclined to coerce us into accepting the thought forms of Scripture as inseparable from the revelation, the existentialist is inclined to absolutize some of the thought forms of modern (existentialist) man, so that we are not to be permitted to hear anything from Scripture that sets them in question. But perhaps the existentialist is too sure, on the one hand, concerning what he thinks he knows of himself, and on the other hand, concerning what he thinks no man can know of God. He may have to rethink all his categories concerning God and man if once he opens his mind and heart to what is meant by God becoming man in Jesus Christ, a miracle that is not likely to have meaning for him until his proud autonomy is broken open and conquered by the same Spirit of God that possessed and indwelt the flesh of Jesus Christ. We are not wise to approach the Scriptures with the assumption that we already have solid knowledge of both God and man, for the claim of Scripture is that here God and man are revealed as nowhere else. Too often in the past, those things which man has assumed too quickly to be the temporary husk of revelation, to be peeled off in order to disclose the abiding truth, have proved eventually to consist of elements in the revelation that were distasteful to the age of the interpreter, yet essential to what that age needed to hear from Scripture. It is necessary, then, that there should be no limitations on the dialogue with Scripture from either side. The relation should be one of unconditional openness. The authority of Scripture is not to be used to limit or restrain or channel the response of modern man; he must have his freedom to question, to react, to deny, or to affirm in his own way. But neither is the authority of what modern man thinks he knows to be used to silence the witness of the Scriptures at any point. If Scripture says that the sun stood still, modern man has a right to question the historical validity of the statement; it is not necessarily true merely because it stands in Scripture. But if modern man is inclined to assert that a resurrection from the dead is impossible, he had better at least consider the possibility that his own assumptions concerning life and death may not yet have taken the full nature of reality into account.

IMPLICATIONS FOR INTERPRETATION

It is essential to a conversation that the partners to it speak a common language. If the Old Testament remained in Hebrew, there would be few persons who would have any idea of what it says. It has been brought at least into the language area of modern man by the excellent translations of it into modern languages. But it is a mistake to think that these alone are sufficient to make it comprehensible. It has its own unique way of speaking which must be learned patiently. It makes demands upon anyone who would enter into conversation with it, not unreasonable demands; in fact, simply the demands that any stranger makes upon us. We must learn how a stranger uses his words and phrases if we are to understand him accurately, especially the peculiar force that he gives to certain words. The Old Testament writer says, " Our God is a consuming fire." He thinks of God's guiding and protecting presence with Israel in the exodus as though it were a visible pillar of fire, appearing as a column of smoke in the daytime and as a fiery pillar in the dark of the night. Ezekiel in his vision of God sees, as it were, a flaming presence, hidden and yet flashing forth from a cloud. Jeremiah feels God's word like fire burning in his bones. This likening of God to fire can easily lead to misunderstanding, especially when the fire is represented as visible to the outward eye, and yet it expresses vividly the reality of the personal presence of the living God to the Israelite.

Again, the prophet Amos says, " God took me from following the flock and said to me: ' Go, prophesy to my people Israel,' " which might well suggest a physical encounter of God with Amos and audible words sounding in his outward ear. But anyone who is familiar with the vivid language of the prophets will understand what a complex of influences and circumstances may lie behind the simple narrative of Amos' call. Or even more open to misunderstanding is the prophetic proclamation of God's coming, his coming in judgment to confront his people with their sins or his coming in mercy to inaugurate a new day for them. But the prophets make it quite sufficiently clear that God's coming to Israel is not a movement in space any more than Israel's return to God is a movement in space. Both movements are in the realm of the spirit, with visible consequences in the world of time and space. But surely it is not too much to ask of any man that he learn the language of the Scriptures so that his conversation with them may not be a broken one in which he catches only fragments of what is being said, but rather, one in which the full depth of the meaning breaks in upon him continually.

A great deal has been written about the hiatus between the Biblical language and the language of modern man and the necessity for a translation of the content of the Scriptures from the one language into the other. The assumption is that modern man now lives in a world in which the Biblical terminology is simply incomprehensible to him. One has therefore to determine the language that *is* comprehensible to him and then translate the essentials of the Biblical witness into that language. But why should modern man be assumed to be so limited in the capacity to understand other languages than his own, or to enter imaginatively into other worlds than his own? He may not enter wholly or understand completely, but if he makes the effort, he can at least begin a conversation with the stranger from another world, a conversation which, as it continues, will become increasingly a way of access. The mind and spirit and actions of the prophet Jeremiah are very strange to the average person in our Western culture. To take just one point, the advice of Jeremiah to his Judean rulers to capitulate to the Babylonians, representing this as God's word of command to his people, is incomprehensible to the patriotic citizen of today. But Jeremiah does not need to remain incomprehensible to him. The way is open for him to get to know this prophet intimately, to see from within what made him speak and act as he did. He may still be puzzled at many points, but at least he will have entered into conversation with a prophet who was unconditionally open toward God and who, with absolute integrity, spoke to his fellow Judeans that which he believed God was saying to them in their embattled situation. It is open to question, therefore, whether there is any need to undertake the vast, complex, and perilous task of translating the content of Scripture out of Biblical terminology into the terminology of the supposedly mature, science-minded man of today. Such a translation is perilous because it is constantly in danger of eliminating those essentials of the content which resist the new terminology. All that is needed is an openness and willingness on the part of our modern man, whatever may be the nature of his mind, to enter into honest conversation with these men of the Biblical world, whose integrity must impress him deeply if he is in truth a man of science.

The relation to one another of the various participants in the

Biblical dialogue sets the pattern for our entrance into the dialogue. They are bound into a unity with one another by their worship and service of the same God. The God of Abraham and the God of Jeremiah is recognizably one and the same God. The word of Amos to Israel is clearly in direct continuity with the word of Nathan to King David more than two centuries earlier. And yet each witness to this word of God speaks with the most complete freedom as a man of his own time to the people of his own time. No prophet — in fact, no Biblical author of any kind — feels any compulsion to be in verbal agreement with any of his predecessors. Each feels only the responsibility to speak God's word with integrity in the unique situation that belongs to him. Certainly the later prophets, such as Ezekiel and Second Isaiah, must have been familiar with the sermons of earlier prophets, but there is not the slightest indication of any inclination on their part to repeat what others had said.

The same freedom is evident in the New Testament. Jesus acknowledged John the Baptist to be a servant of the same Word of God by which he lived, and yet he stubbornly refused to let pious men force him into a conformity of word and practice with John. So also Paul claimed a unity with Jesus Christ so intense that he could say that Christ lived afresh in him, and yet when he came to preach the gospel to the people of his world he had to say everything differently from the way in which Jesus himself had spoken, so differently that many able scholars have thought that he was preaching a different gospel. This points the way for us. When we enter into the goodly fellowship of the prophets and the apostles we become servants together with them of the Word they served, bound to it as they were bound, and we become sharers with them in both the responsibility and the freedom of speaking the same word with integrity in the very different language and situation of our modern world.

RESPONSIBILITY AND FREEDOM

The responsibility and the freedom are inseparable. The freedom is not license to put forward whatever thoughts the prophets and apostles inspire in us and to call them the modern version of the prophetic and apostolic word. We are free to speak and act as men of the twentieth century, not parroting the words of some earlier century or copying the actions of some authentic servant of God of the past, but saying and doing what God gives us to say and do with all our heart and mind and strength *now*. But, like the prophets and apostles, we are able to have such freedom only because we are bound unconditionally to God as he has revealed himself consistently in the life of his people in the past and as he continues to be known through the record that bears witness to that revelation. That means that we are bound to the Scriptures, bound to speak no other word than the one that comes to utterance there. Yet because we are bound not by the letter but by the Spirit, not by the external form of the words but by the Word of life that sounds in the words, we are endowed by this Word and Spirit with freedom to be faithful witnesses in our own century.

The test, then, of any modern interpretation of Scripture is whether in it the same word from God that once sounded into an ancient world is actually to be heard in the modern world. But if it is the same word, we would expect that there would be some correspondence between the impact then and the impact now. That consideration is a sobering one for all who have to do with the interpretation of Scripture — not just professors of theology but also preachers and teachers in the churches. Interpreting the word of God in Scripture is so often a very tame affair, so much so that the suggestion that it might be dangerous is likely to seem ridiculous. Yet these words in their original historical situation were frequently highly dangerous, involving their spokesmen in all manner of trouble and at times demanding that they set their very lives in jeopardy. Looking back, we may find it to be an almost terrifying task that these men undertook, to speak to the men of their time a word of God that was a matter of life or death for those who heard it. In comparison our own task of Biblical interpretation seems to us much more modest and commonplace and safe. But how can it be so if the goal of our interpretation is that the same living Word of God that was heard then is actually to be heard through us today? Our task is no less venturesome, no less awesome, no less dangerous.

Perhaps what frequently makes interpretation a tame affair is that the attention is concentrated wholly upon the explication of the text to the neglect of the situation of the present-day hearer. The interpreter proceeds as though the problems were all in the Biblical text and his task were finished when he has offered a clear and valid exegesis of it, when actually that is only preparation for the dialogue. The exegesis is wasted unless what was originally said begins to be heard now, and the problem of the hearing is as complex and difficult and worthy of careful investigation as the problem of the exegesis. Both partners to the dialogue have to be taken seriously and brought into active participation. The hearer brings to the text of Scripture, not a passive mind that has only to receive impressions and to take in the words, but rather, a total existence that is already moving in a certain direction on the basis of certain convictions.

To begin at the surface level, the hearer has a vocabulary in which words have definite meanings that are not likely to correspond very closely with the meanings these words have in Scripture, so that the very words of Scripture convey to him something other than their true meaning until somehow they are reminted in his mind and experience. What is it to him to love, to be meek, to have faith? The image called up in his mind by the word " God " may have little in common with the God of the prophets. But beneath all this is the fact that in the Scriptures he comes into encounter with the records of faith not as one who has no faith but as one who, even though he is a Christian, is activated by a faith that is in many respects contrary to what is revealed in the Scriptures as true faith. He cannot be a responsible human being without having some convictions about what it means to be a man, but when the prophets and Jesus and Paul begin to define his humanity for him he is likely to find many of his most cherished convictions set in question. He has an understanding of his world that he has drawn from different quarters, but there is a uniquely Biblical understanding of the world as God's creation that is likely to make him rethink many things that he has taken for granted.

The Bible is not heard in a vacuum. The territory into which it sounds is already occupied. God lays claim to men who have already been claimed by other gods, and have already committed themselves to another pattern of life than that which is inherent in a life in covenant with God. A simpler way to say it is that we always enter into dialogue with Scripture as sinners and unbelievers who may expect to hear a word that cuts across their whole way of life like a sharp two-edged sword and who may also expect their minds to try every possible device to evade the sharpness of the voice they hear. Therefore, to hear is always to be confronted with an ultimate decision in which one's very existence is in the balances.

One might be inclined to ask what hope there is of men hearing the message of the Scriptures however faithfully we preach and teach it if their minds are constantly drawing wrong meanings from the words and if their sin and unbelief makes them in self-protection instinctively misunderstand what is being said. The answer is that they will never understand if the word of God never meets them in any other form than as the words of a book. God did not entrust his word in the Old Testament primarily to a book, but to a people who were to let themselves be possessed, guided, comforted, and ruled by it in the entirety of their lives. The sacred records were preserved merely that this people might never forget the word in which alone they had their life. So also in the New Testament the Word of God had to be spelled out in the flesh of Jesus Christ in order to get past the obstacles in men's existences. The love of God could be known in its reality only as it was interpreted in the person of Jesus Christ and then through him in the persons of those who were united with him in faith. There had to be, and there has to be, a people of God whose life is shaped by its hearing and answering the word that meets it in the Scriptures and that reaches out, past the sin and unbelief and misunderstanding of men, to confront them with a living embodiment of the gospel. This confrontation takes the form of a dialogue. Honest words are spoken, and the answers, whether questioning and hostile or eager and inquiring, are met with more honest words, the modern continuation of the dialogue that has its source in Scripture and that by its very nature leads ever back to find its own mysterious and life-giving depths in Scripture.

II

CREATOR, CREATION, AND CREATURES

THE FIRST CHAPTER of Genesis is written in the simplest words, yet contains very important, though also very obscure, matters. Therefore, according to Saint Jerome, it was forbidden to anyone among the Jews to read or explain it to others before he had reached the age of thirty years. They held that whoever was to read or understand the first chapter of Genesis should first of all have understood, studied, and digested all the Sacred Scriptures." Those are the words with which Martin Luther begins his preface to his commentary on Genesis. Like all the Reformers he was conscious of profoundly important truth being embodied in the early chapters of Genesis, and anyone who is familiar with the sixteenth- and seventeenth-century Protestant confessions of faith will know how the doctrines of man's creation in the image of God and of his fall from grace form the setting in which Christ's work of redemption is interpreted. But Luther was also conscious of how easily men could be led astray in their understanding of these chapters, so that they entangled the truth contained in them with all manner of absurdities.

It is interesting to read both Luther and Calvin on this first chapter of Genesis and to compare their dialogue with it to our own. Nothing could make clearer to us that each generation must conduct its own dialogue with Scripture, since it simply does not hear the text with the same ears that belonged to even the wisest and most venerable of the fathers. Frequently we find in Luther and Calvin insights into the meaning of Scripture that are most enlightening, but elsewhere we are reminded forcefully that four hundred years have passed since they wrote. Both Reformers read this chapter in Genesis as a literal description of how the world came into being. Calvin asserts that no sane person would doubt that Adam was well instructed about the origin of the world and that beginning with him, this knowledge was carefully passed on from generation to generation until eventually Moses wrote it down. He also suggests that since Moses could look forward to future events, he must also have been able to look back to past events, even to those before the creation of man. Both Calvin and Luther assumed that the earth was at the center of all things and that the sun, moon, stars, and the whole of the heavens rotated at a great speed around the earth. Luther marvels that they are not burned up by the speed of their rotation.

Two things are clear, then, when we consider what this chapter meant to the Reformers. On the one hand, they brought to it minds that cannot any longer be the minds of honest modern men. There is no accusation in this against the intelligence or integrity of the Reformers. They were men of the highest intelligence and integrity who simply shared the limitations of knowledge of the men of their day just as we share in the limitations of the knowledge of our day. But no man can any longer think that the sun revolves around the earth or that the earth is the center of the universe or that the world was created in 4004 B.C. and be either intelligent or honest. On the other hand, we must recognize that, in spite of the Reformers' reading the chapter as a play-by-play account of the events of Creation and in spite of what seems to us an amazing naïveté, they nevertheless heard the essential message of the chapter with a remarkable clarity, and the Biblical doctrine of God the Creator, of the world as God's creation, and of man as a creature in God's likeness entered into the structure of their thought and became basic to their approach to life in a way that, I am afraid, is no longer true of us. We have become more sophisticated in our reading of Genesis and are unlikely to be guilty of any of the naïve interpretations of the Reformers, but somehow we no longer believe in God as the Creator and Sovereign of our world as they did, nor do we wait upon him to restore in us his own likeness and image as they did.

The Relation of Creation to Redemption

There is a remark of Luther in the passage that I quoted at the beginning which is well worth our attention, the remark that he who would understand the first chapter of Genesis needs to have studied and digested all the Sacred Scriptures. Gerhard von Rad in his recent excellent commentary on Genesis makes a somewhat similar statement, pointing out that the story of Creation cannot be understood in isolation from the total context in which it stands in the Pentateuch as a whole. In both the Yahwist and the Priestly document, faith in salvation and election is central, and " they undergird this faith by the testimony that this Yahweh, who made a covenant with Abraham and at Sinai, is also the creator of the world." The fact that the story of Creation stands first in the Bible leads constantly to misunderstanding, giving the impression that belief in God the Creator is the beginning point in a Biblical faith or a Biblical theology. The same impression is conveyed by the Apostles' Creed, as though one should be able to confess his faith in God the Father Almighty, Maker of heaven and earth, before ever he knows anything of God's saving and reconciling power in Jesus Christ. Far too often the church has been misled by this in its preaching and teaching, assuming that the order in which to proceed is first to bring men to believe in God and then on that foundation to build their faith in Jesus Christ. We need to ponder the statement that occurs in slightly different forms in the Gospel of Matthew and the Gospel of John, that no one can rightly know the Father except through the Son, that is, that we do not rightly know the meaning of these words " God," " Father," " Almighty," and " Creator " until they are spelled out for us by what God is to us in and through Jesus Christ. To put it in theological terms: knowledge of God as our Redeemer comes first, and only in the light of that knowledge can we rightly know him as Creator and Father.

So also in the Old Testament it is a fact that in the history of

Israel, faith in God as Creator came not first but second. First was the covenant relation between God and Israel, God's election of Israel, his choice of this people to stand in a unique personal relationship with himself, his disclosure to Israel of his own nature and purpose and of the nation's destiny as the instrument of his purpose among men. Israel knew God in his word as Judge and Redeemer in the present moment in history, as the One who not only had called them into being as a nation but was constantly the determiner of their destiny in the present and future. Their only possibility of a future was through faithfulness in their covenant relation with him. Because he was sovereign, his will compassed all things in their life, and, as they recognized the universal scope of his sovereignty, the whole world became the stage for the unfolding of his purpose. The fulfillment of that purpose was not to be in some realm above and beyond this world, but rather, in the midst of human affairs and human history. Therefore when they looked back to the beginning of things, asking deep questions about the origin of the world and of human life, the answers they found were determined by what they knew of God as the living, present Lord and Redeemer of men. They confessed that he by his word brought into being an ordered world where at first there had been only chaos because not just once but many times in their history they had known his power to conquer life's chaos with his word and to create a future where none had seemed to be possible. A prophet such as Second Isaiah lives and breathes in the confidence that God *is* the Creator, not just that once long ago he *was* the Creator. All hope for the future of a scattered Israel facing the most depressing circumstances resided in the power of God to bring into being an order of life vastly different from the existing one.

We are warned therefore not to deal with the account of Creation in isolation, as though it were a specimen of early Hebrew speculation about the origin of all things. Nor should we encourage anyone to think that he should be able to arrive at faith in God the Creator by merely contemplating the Creation. There is a long history in the Christian church of attempts to deduce a

Creator God from the structure and character of the universe. The stately Gifford Lectures in Scotland were instituted for the specific purpose of encouraging this kind of theological endeavor. More familiar to us, however, is the popular refrain in preaching and in educational materials: "The creation mirrors the Creator. Look to nature with an open and responsive mind and heart and you will find God." Not long ago it was thought that one of the best ways in which "to give children and youth an experience of God" was to expose them to the beauties of nature, at the same time suggesting softly to them that what they were feeling in response to the beauty was none other than the presence of God. It was not realized that such a procedure was more likely to produce pantheists, pagan nature worshipers, or, through radical disillusionment, outright atheists. But all we need to say at this point is that the Scriptures nowhere lead us to expect that by the contemplation of nature we may arrive at faith in *this* God, the God of Israel and the God and Father of Jesus Christ. The philosophers of Greece and India, with brilliant minds and earnestness of purpose, peered into the phenomena of life for a very long time and came to the unanimous conclusion that they must despair of any purpose or ultimate meaning in the material world. Why did Israel not share that despair? It was not because of a more effective contemplation of nature, but rather, because of their ever-renewed confrontation in the midst of life with a word from God in which God revealed his power to transform the character of the human situation. They believed in God as Creator because in their present situation they knew his creative and redemptive power in his word.

THE FREEDOM WITH WHICH WE READ

We take up our dialogue, then, with Gen., ch. 1, and the first thing we do is establish our right to hear it with twentieth-century ears, while at the same time we concede to the author the right to speak as the inhabitant of a prescientific age. It is strange that the church has been so slow in recognizing these corresponding rights of author and reader. The relation between the two has

frequently been frozen into unreality by the insistence either that
the ancient author should be held to say nothing but what is intellectually up to date in the twentieth century or that the twentieth-century reader should identify himself with an intellectual
outlook that belongs to the fifth century B.C. Author and reader
must both be liberated, the one to speak and the other to hear,
each as a person of integrity in his own time. Perhaps the anxiety
and timidity with which many a modern reader enters the sacred domain of Scripture arises from the fact that he has not
been adequately confirmed in that freedom, to hear as a twentieth-century man, so that when he finds his twentieth-century
mind questioning things that seem to be stated as facts in Scripture, it frightens him and makes him either draw back and leave
the Bible alone or decide in his mind that its contents are not
really true.

I would raise the question seriously whether the church of our
day in its preaching and teaching takes account of the fact that
even a child of nine or ten years of age finds this problem inescapable. Does he get any help with it from his church or his
church school? His school books in history, geography, and science acquaint him with the dimensions of the universe in time
and space. He knows that the earth is only a tiny speck in a vast
universe, that beyond the blue of the sky are infinite regions of
space, and stars larger than our sun are millions of light-years
away. He knows that the story of man began several hundred
thousand years ago and that the civilizations of six thousand
years with which we are acquainted are only the final episode in
the life of man. Yet frequently the story of Creation is presented
by the churches to that child and youth, and to his parents, as
though they were able to hear it as naïvely as men did as recently
as four centuries ago, when actually their perplexity with it is so
great that they can no longer hear it saying anything to them at
all. How many ten-year-olds, observing the contradictions between their school books and Genesis and hearing nothing from
the church about how such difficulties are to be resolved, quietly
decide in their own minds that what is in the Bible is not really

true and that the authority of the scientist and the schoolteacher takes precedence over the authority of the Bible and the church? Let him have his freedom to belong to his own century and then teach him to read with respect the confessions of faith of people who lived in a prescientific age. Nothing could be healthier for him than to learn that on the deeper questions of life some of these ancient Hebrews knew so much more than we do that we have to sit humbly at their feet and be taught by them. We may be beyond them in scientific knowledge, but in the understanding of God and man and the meaning of life in this world, they are beyond us in such a way that we can never overtake them.

It is a shock at first for many people to realize that the author of Gen., ch. 1, thought of the world as a kind of flat island, firmly anchored in place but floating on a great ocean that surrounded it on every side and with a solid, transparent firmament like an inverted bowl above it, through which, in the daytime could be seen the blue waters of a celestial ocean, and in the nighttime the moon and the stars. But any fair-minded person must recognize that that is approximately the way the world appears to a person who has only his two eyes and no telescope with which to look and who has traveled only far enough from home to discover that every direction leads eventually to a sea. Naturally it was not yet known to him that the light in which the earth is bathed in daytime and which is reflected back upon the earth from the moon in nighttime has its source wholly in the sun, so that he could describe light as existing before there was a sun. Darkness seemed to him an entity as substantial as light and not just an absence of light, so that he could speak of darkness and light as being divided from each other and assigned to different portions of the day. To depreciate all that the author says because he embodies in his statements conceptions such as these, which seem so childishly primitive to us, is the mark of an undiscriminating mind that shuts itself off from the wisdom of the ancient world by its inability to discern where a man merely expresses the limitations of the knowledge of his time and where he breaks through those limitations to command the attention of men of every age.

That the first act of Creation is God's calling into being a light to shine in the darkness has theological significance. In Isa. 60:19 the prophet envisages a day when the sun and moon will have vanished but the whole creation will be resplendent in the light that shines from God's own presence. The light of Gen. 1:3 is an element of the Creation and not the light of the divine glory, but it is the indispensable element that forms the background of the whole work of Creation. Analogous to this is God's creative work in man's redemption in which the illumination of his existence by God's word stands at the very beginning.

THE PRIMACY OF GOD

What, then, does this ancient author say to us? First, he says that this world in which we find ourselves does not exist of itself and does not have the secret of its life within itself. The world is not eternal; it is a creation that has a beginning and an end and its history unfolds between that beginning and end. The primary reality is not the world that seems so solid and substantial but the everlasting God upon whom all things depend for their existence. He speaks his word and they emerge out of chaos; he withdraws his word and they perish. This is not speculation; it is a confession of faith, the confession that is made not only here at the beginning of the Old Testament but by a succession of prophets, priests, psalmists, and wise men all the way through. Moreover, it is the confession, not of religious mystics meditating on God in a secluded corner where they are protected from the ordinary experiences of life, but of men who are turned outward toward the world and are peculiarly sensitive to the whole range of problems with which human existence is plagued. We become aware of a vast difference between these confessors and ourselves as we listen to them. For us, the world and man are the substantial realities, so that we start from them and try to think our way up to God. But these men do just the opposite. For them, *God* is the substantial reality, so that the world and man are set in question; they begin with God and think their way down to the world and man.

We may as well face the fact that it is here at this central point and not on the periphery that modern man, and in many instances modern theologians, are in basic disagreement with the Old Testament. They are affronted that the Hebrew theologian should take this bold step and should dare to begin with God and not with man. It has become an axiom in some forms of existentialist thinking that man's knowledge extends only to the limits of his human existence, so that he can know God only indirectly as the reality of God is reflected in the changes that take place in his human self-understanding. Or God is posited as the ultimate ground of being that is disclosed when the human mind penetrates the ambiguities of existence to discern the reality that lies at the source of everything. It seems only reasonable to most men that if there is a God, the surest clues to his nature should be discernible in the universe itself and in the life of man. Man must take himself and his world as the starting point. How can he leap beyond himself to start from God? The answer of the Hebrew theologian is that he does not leap beyond himself; he simply knows himself to be addressed from beyond the limits of his own existence by One who binds him to Himself and in binding him sets him free to live. His own will is encountered from the Beyond by a will that, on the one hand, contradicts it and, on the other, affirms for it possibilities of life that of itself it would never dare to claim. God has spoken to him out of the unseen, not just on some single historical occasion that might be dismissed as an instance of ancient superstition, but generation after generation, alongside, and in the midst of, the common events of life. Century after century there were in Israel these ears that were open to a voice out of the unseen, and there came into being a cumulative body of historical witness, consistent in its character, concerning the nature of the mind and will with which Israel had to deal. The testimony of Israel's most sensitive and honest spirits, never merely parroting the words of predecessors, but each speaking of what he knows in accents that suggest the utmost personal integrity, is that the center not only of Israel's life but also of each individual's life and of the life of humanity is in the unseen, in a God who claims for himself absolute mastery over the world's existence.

What is more striking to the modern reader than the assurance with which the Old Testament speaks of God? " In the beginning God created the heavens and the earth "; " God is our refuge and strength "; " The Lord is my shepherd "; " The earth is the Lord's and the fulness thereof "; " Have you not known? Have you not heard? The Lord is the everlasting God, the Creator of the ends of the earth. He does not faint or grow weary, his understanding is unsearchable." These men speak of a God whom they know, and their entire understanding of themselves and their entire approach to life is determined by what they know of God. They know him because he has disclosed himself uniquely in Israel's life in a word by which he first established a personal relation between himself and Israel and then through which he has continued at each step in history to illumine the relation. The validation of this word has been that a response to it in trust and obedience has given meaning and purpose to life even in the most difficult circumstances, while deafness to it and rebellion against it have constantly issued in self-destructiveness. These men do not attempt to prove the truth of their statements concerning God, nor do they ask anyone to accept the statements on their authority. Their constant assumption is that anyone can know what they know if he is willing to let his blindness and deafness, that is, his personal resistance to God, be overcome. Since God has bound man to himself, has made him so that he cannot have his true life as man except in fellowship with God, how could it be otherwise than that the reality of God should, in each moment, be impinging upon the life of man? Man's dilemma is not that he cannot find God, but rather, that he cannot get free of God. What he calls his search for God is really a search for some other god than the one who constantly presses upon him such seemingly intolerable claims that in loyalty to his own self-sovereignty he feels compelled to deny him. The ultimate problem in knowing God is not primarily an intellectual one, but rather, whether one is willing to acknowledge that at the base of life is a personal relation in which the will of God is absolutely sovereign and man finds his freedom to live by taking his place as a subject, and not a master, in the realm of his sovereign.

There is another aspect from which perhaps we can understand this confession. In the ancient world as in the modern world, nothing was more obvious than that a large portion of the conflicts and oppressions that brought suffering and disorder into human society had their origin in the covetousness of men and nations, their inordinate desire to take possession of the earth. The prophets of Israel encountered it in the efforts of successful merchants and nobles to build large estates for themselves even though it meant dispossessing peasants who had a time-honored claim to the land. It was evident also in the constant temptation of the nation's rulers to extend their power and to enrich themselves at the expense of the common people. But it came to its most forceful expression in the activities of the great world powers of Mesopotamia and Egypt, whose attempts to establish their sovereignty over ever larger areas of the earth had from time immemorial had such painful and disastrous consequences for the smaller nations such as Israel whose territories lay in between. Man tries to take possession of the earth by force but it eludes him, for what he grasps in his hand turns out to be but an empty shell. Why does he fail in his drive for possession? What he does not know is that the earth belongs to God and is to be possessed by man only as God's gift to him in trust. The gateway to the true possession of the earth is not by force but by a faith in which man takes the place that is assigned to him by God. The psalmist says that " the meek shall inherit the earth," and by " the meek " he does not mean a slavishly submissive person, but rather, one who is utterly humbled before the majesty of God, that is, one who has become willing to let God alone be sovereign.

The Word That Conquers Chaos

There are arguments among scholars as to whether the word for " create " in v. 1 signifies of itself " to create out of nothing."

Some hold that in the Old Testament it is reserved for God's sovereign creative act that calls into being that which was not there before, never being used to describe man's shaping of material. Others disagree. But there can surely be no disagreement that the intention of the author was to make all things that exist dependent upon the creative power of God. In the beginning there is only God, and then by God's creative act there is a world and man. That the world exists at first as a watery mass in which there is no order and no life is not intended to suggest an eternally preexisting matter independent of God and eternally resistant to God, an idea that would introduce a basic dualism into the Biblical faith. Rather, this primordial chaos represents the dark disorder that constantly threatens the life of man. The story of the Flood graphically portrays a return of the world to chaos as a consequence of man's rebellion against the rule of God. In succeeding ages it is only God's faithfulness to his purpose and his compassion for man that prevents a new inbreaking of the floods. In the exile the Jews eventually came to feel that God had abandoned them because of their sins, so that their life was engulfed in darkness, but Second Isaiah assured them that He who formed the earth did not create it to be a chaos (Isa. 45:18). But the threat is there, and in a modern atomic age the threat is most ominously there. The will of the Creator is that chaos should be conquered, that an ordered world in which man finds blessing should exist, and not a chaos. What is it that lets man despairingly slip back into chaos, folding his hands as though he could do nothing about it, except that in his eagerness to be sovereign of the world himself, he has become blind to the Creator who alone has power to speak the word that conquers chaos.

In our emphasizing that God alone can speak the word that brings order out of chaos, let us not forget, however, that this is the very word that he calls man to speak for him. In Second Isaiah the word which God has hidden in the life of his servant people is likened to rain or snow that falls from heaven upon the desert of life to transform it and to make it fruitful (Isa. 55:10-11), or to a sharp sword with which God overcomes his enemies

(Isa. 49:2). In Ps. 8 the insignificance of man in the midst of God's majestic creation is balanced by his amazing destiny: that in his mouth God sets the word that "stills the enemy and the avenger" (Ps. 8:2). The word entrusted to Israel that has in it power to create a new heaven and a new earth is the same word by means of which God first called an ordered world into being. We shall have to weigh the significance of this for our understanding of what it means for man to be created in the likeness of God. When is he more truly a reflection of God than when he is the servant and the bearer of God's word, not only bearing it upon his lips but shaped by it in his inmost being? We may well remember that the Second Adam, who was "the express image of the Father," was the incarnation of the word of God and the promise of a new creation.

MAN IN GOD'S IMAGE

No single element in the Creation story has been so variously interpreted as the making of man in God's image. The usual attempt is to find something in man's nature as an individual that can be identified with the image of God in him. Some say that it is his reason; there he seems to them to come closest to the divine. Others say that it was in his bodily form that man was thought to resemble God; still others that it was some spiritual quality in him. The most widespread idea is that it represents a divine element, many would say a divine spark, that resides in man as man. So firmly fixed is this last conception in the minds even of children that this is what they hear when Gen. 1:26-27 is read to them. And yet if there is one thing that it cannot mean, it is this. No Hebrew prophet or priest would ever have been guilty of endowing man with a divine spark. For the Hebrew, God is a person who enters into personal relation with man, not some kind of impersonal spark hidden away in the recesses of man's being to be discovered by him and fanned into a blaze. For him, God is God and man is man. God is Creator and man is creature, which means that man is not God, not divine in any way. As Ecclesiastes puts it, "God is in heaven and thou upon earth." There is no divinizing of man in the Scriptures, neither in the Old nor in the New Testament.

I would suggest to you that there is no greater obstacle to the hearing of the gospel in any Christian congregation than the conviction of men, nourished from many sources, that they are already in some degree divine, nor is there any more fertile cause of dividedness and confusion of soul than the contradiction between this sentimental and romantic delusion and the actuality of man's concrete existence. I would suggest too that there is no better remedy for such delusions than a hearing of the Old Testament on the subject of man's creatureliness and man's place in the midst of creation. But we shall consider this further in the next chapter.

What, then, does it mean that man is made in God's likeness? The fact that he is created on the sixth day, together with all the animals that people the earth, seems to take account of what he shares with the animal creation. But his unique destiny is that he is to maintain order in the creation on God's behalf. He is to rule for God. He is to be the instrument of God's purpose in the history that is to unfold, but that is possible only if the very nature of God is reflected in his nature. To rule for God he must be just, as God is just; holy, as God is holy; true, as God is true; faithful, as God is faithful. For him to be unjust, unholy, untrue, unfaithful, would be for him to cease to reflect God's nature and so to become the creator of disorder, rather than of order, upon the earth. The likeness, then, is not something that man can claim as an intrinsic excellence of his nature, but rather, exists in him only insofar as he is what God created him to be, the partner of his purpose, the bearer of his word, a creature responding in love to the love that has chosen him for such a glorious destiny. Cut off from that destiny by his own willfulness and separated from God, he ceases to reflect the nature of God, but nothing he can do will make him other than a creature who was created for such a destiny as that.

The Goodness of the Creation

There is one thing more that must be mentioned because of its great importance: the recurrent note that when God looked upon what he had made he saw that it was good. We live in a time when the outlook for humanity is so grim that stark pessimism infiltrates the souls of men. They are susceptible to it perhaps because they come from a time when they indulged themselves in a superficial optimism about the world. A Biblical faith lies beyond both optimism and pessimism. It looks with open eyes into the full tragedy of human life, concealing nothing. It lays bare the dread potentialities of evil that reside in even the best and most religious men. But never can it be misled into a negation of the world and the flesh such as we find in Greek and Indian thought, so that God has to be sought by some manner of flight from the world. What people ever experienced the horror and agony that can be the lot of men and nations more fully than Israel? And yet they held fast to the conviction that in God's sight the world is good! Where it is evil, it is man who has made it evil. In itself it is good, the creation of God's loving purpose, chosen by him as the scene of man's redemption. Directly in line with this is the sanctifying of our human existence by Jesus' sharing of it with us, himself the very incarnation of God, and making of us, as Paul says, temples of the Holy Spirit. A Biblical faith takes the world and the flesh with the utmost seriousness and approaches it with the utmost reverence because the purpose of the Creator was not to dwell in majesty in some lofty heaven far off from his creation but to dwell in the midst of his creatures, making of them a family for himself on earth and guiding them through the tangled paths of history toward the fulfillment of his purpose for them.

III

THE PROBLEM OF HUMAN NATURE
AND DESTINY

WHEN WE TURN from the Priestly story of Creation in ch. 1 of Genesis to the more ancient story in chs. 2 and 3, we are impressed at once by the concentration of the interest upon man. The one story represents in broad, bold strokes the creation and ordering of a world with the appearance of man in the final act to show the meaning and purpose of it all. The other lets the world at large fade quickly into the background and focuses the entire attention upon man. It betrays a very great concern about what we would call the human dilemma. Man as we left him in ch. 1 was literally sitting on top of the world — created in God's likeness to rule for him over the whole creation. But the earlier tradition in chs. 2 and 3 has a much more subdued tone. What is man but a handful of dust into which God has breathed the breath of life? That he should be alive at all is a miracle. But alive he is and haunted by the suspicion that the world as he experiences it is not the world as it was intended to be and that he himself has somehow missed his destiny. He has woman as his companion to comfort his loneliness, but he is inclined to blame her for all his troubles. But his deepest dilemma is that his relationship with God, which should have been his greatest strength and joy, is broken and darkened, making him feel himself guilty and cursed instead of blessed, and with the prospect before him of a long and uncertain struggle with forces hostile to him.

It is this subdued, troubled, and questioning tone that is likely to catch the ear of modern man because he too is engrossed by the human dilemma. The threat of atomic destruction makes him acutely aware of how quickly a large portion of humanity could be reduced to little heaps of dust. Convinced that he has the technical know-how to make the earth a paradise, he finds himself somehow turning it into a hell. Marriage, the most intimate relationship of life, seems to promise so much but becomes frequently a source of misery and disaster and ends in divorce. Why do things go wrong as they do in spite of man's best intentions? And perhaps modern man, if he were really honest, would agree with the author of Gen., chs. 2 and 3, that he is much more conscious of the curse of God than of the blessing of God resting upon him. He is a painful problem to himself. Perhaps, then, he may be willing to listen to an ancient probing of that painful problem.

The Mythological Barrier

The chief obstacle in the way of a fruitful dialogue between these chapters and modern man is that the ancient tradition has gathered into it so many mythological elements that are strange and perplexing to the mind in an unmythological age such as ours. We want plain, unvarnished fact and truth. A myth for us usually means something that is untrue rather than an imaginative and childlike expression that may embody in its own way more truth than our unvarnished facts. Mythology also suggests primitive superstition to us. Therefore when we find so much that is mythological in these chapters we are inclined to dismiss them as primitive and superstitious. It must be admitted frankly that they are crowded with mythological features. God is pictured as one who shapes the dampened earth with his hands to form a man, who performs an operation on man in order to secure the rib out of which to make a woman, and who goes walking in the garden in the cool of the day. The garden has one tree in it whose fruit confers immortality and another that gives knowledge of good and evil. There is a serpent that stands upright and talks, and there are cherubim who guard the gates of the garden with flaming swords. These are not features that encourage thoughtful men today to expect from such a document a serious and important communication of truth. They find it hard to approach the originators of the document with respect and openness. It sounds to them more like a fairy story than a divine revelation. What they need to grasp, however, is that the naïveté is in the language and the images and not in the understanding of God and man which the language and images are used to express. When we read these chapters aright we find ourselves in the presence of one of the profoundest theologians of all time. One has only to think of the shelves of books that have been written and are still being written to explore the depth of meaning in these writings of the tenth century B.C. Who else from the tenth or ninth or eighth century B.C. apart from this Hebrew theologian still commands that kind of attention? He probed the problem of man to the depths and expressed what he found in the only language that he knew — the rich, imaginative language of mythology.

It is wrong, however, to speak of the story itself as a myth. Some have called it a saga. But actually we need a special word of some kind to categorize it adequately. The author has his eye on man, not any one man but humanity as a whole as represented in the man and woman of the story, not some mythical figure of antiquity but in a very realistic way the man whom he knows in himself and his neighbor. The closest likeness to what the author does here, embodying the story of all humanity in the figures of an original man and woman, is actually to be found in Jesus' parable of the prodigal. The prodigal is every man in his relation with God, and the parable is intended to be a mirror in which every man who hears it may see his own face and recognize the reality of his own relation with God. In a similar way our story, although not in the specific form of a parable, has actually this intention of disclosing to every man and woman the truth about themselves. It can lead only to misunderstanding to describe such a document as a myth. It is full to the brim with mythological language and images, but the use made of them is not naïve but, rather, highly sophisticated. This is specially evident in Gen. 3:15, where the history of the descendants of Adam and Eve is likened to an endless battle between humanity and the power of evil represented by the serpent, a battle in which each in turn does damage to the other. Man is given no hope of escaping the sting of the serpent, but he is promised times when the serpent's head will be under his heel.

We should recognize also that the author has not taken the trouble to make all the materials that enter into his story fit neatly together. In ch. 2:6 the earth is watered by a mist that comes up out of it, but in ch. 2:10 there is a river originating in the garden that divides into four rivers and waters the whole earth. In ch. 2:9 and ch. 3:22 there are two trees that must remain untouched, the tree of the knowledge of good and evil and the tree of life, but in three other verses, chs. 2:17; 3:3; and 3:17, there is only one tree whose fruit is forbidden to man. There is also the difficulty that ch. 2:17 seems to presuppose a story in which man is pictured as originally immortal but as bringing death upon himself by his disobedience, while ch. 3:22 suggests a Promethean theme in which man, having snatched for himself the knowledge of good and evil that is reserved for heavenly beings, threatens to eat of the tree of life and become himself an immortal god. Thus we catch glimpses through such cracks in the story into a strange world of ancient myths, but it is neither practicable nor fruitful to attempt their reconstruction out of the fragments that are embodied in the present text. Rather, our concern is with the text as we have it, put together in its present form not by accident but in order to bring to expression a profound understanding of man's nature and destiny. Our primary interest is not in the original form of the traditions that have entered into the story but in the way in which the prophetic mind molds them and makes of them a cunning instrument with which to reveal man to himself.

The Vision of Paradise

Perhaps now we are ready to hear what this ancient theologian has to say to us concerning ourselves. He has a theme that should seize the interest of young and old alike — man, the secret history of how man came to be what he is. He does not solve the dilemma of man. He takes us only partway. Comparing his story with Jesus' story of the prodigal, you might say that he traces the journey of the prodigal only until he is feeding on husks in the far country, and makes no attempt to portray his return home. And yet he manages to suggest to us what life would be were man once more to find where he truly belongs.

The setting of the story is Eden, the garden of God. At once our minds conceive a paradise, but actually we are told very little about Eden. Its situation is vague. It seems to be located somewhere near the sources of the Tigris and Euphrates Rivers. Waters rise from within it to flow out in four streams over the whole earth and make it fruitful. Trees of all kinds provide the necessary food for man. But the primary feature of its life is the simplicity, unbrokenness, and intimacy of man's relation with God, so completely unbroken that it is a state of innocency. Hermann Gunkel, years ago, taught us to see the close connection between this Eden at the beginning of human history and a similar Eden that the prophets envisaged as the goal of history. The definition of the origin of man is at the same time the definition of his ultimate destiny. One paradise, a lost paradise, lies behind him, but there is another paradise that God sets before him as the hope of his future. He loses paradise in the third chapter of Genesis but he is haunted by the memory of it all the way through history. Palestine as the land of promise in the Pentateuch and in Joshua takes on some of the aspects of paradise, a puzzling phenomenon to us in the light of the actualities of Palestinian life until we realize that the journey of the fathers to Palestine had become for a later age a symbolic representation of the journey of Israel through history to the promised goal of human life. This pilgrimage of the people of God through time is perfectly described in Hebrews when it is said of Abraham that he went out not knowing whither he was going but seeking a city that has foundations whose maker and builder is God.

Shall we put this down, then, as merely a beautiful dream with which the Hebrews, and the early Christians, tantalized themselves, the dream of a paradise lost long ago and of a paradise one day to be regained? Or is this a primary assertion of faith, the immediate consequence of man's confrontation with God? The paradise that he places at the beginning and end of history represents the world of which he has a vision when the mind and purpose of God burst in upon him like a blaze of light in the midst of darkness. His whole perspective upon the immediate world is determined by his seeing it always over against the world of God's intention. The brutal world he faces day by day where men lust and hate and steal and kill is not the world that God intended. It is a world that has lost its way. Men can be content to compromise with its ways and make their peace with it only by subduing and banishing the vision of the city that has foundations. In the Gospels the vision of paradise is the vision of the Kingdom, no longer just a distant goal at the end of history but a new world pressing in upon man now, conquering the lust and hate and greed that deface his life and enabling him to live already in joyful anticipation of the fulfillment that is to come.

The vision of paradise is therefore no empty dream or mere speculation of the religious mind. Rather, it is intrinsic to the Biblical vision of God. A God who is just and holy cannot forever endure injustice and unholiness in a world that belongs to him. The goodness and mercy of God cannot forever be restrained by the blind and evil resistance of men. If God be God, then the vindication of his sovereignty demands a world in which his purpose triumphs. The prayer, " Thy kingdom come, thy will be done on earth as it is in heaven " may be answered only in part in each age in history, but the day must come when it is answered fully, when the Kingdom comes and God's will is done on earth. An endless struggle between God and evil in which evil proves as eternal as God himself is a Zoroastrian dualism and could not hold its place in the theology either of a Hebrew prophet or of a Christian apostle, for both of whom the foundation of confidence is the absolute sovereignty of God. A faith in which human existence is laid open unconditionally to God's rule experiences at least the beginnings of the creation of a new order in life and breathes something of the air of God's glorious new world, only a beginning and only a foretaste, yet sufficient to instill an eternal discontent with any lesser order or any other world.

In this context we begin perhaps to grasp the significance of the fact that our author places the humanity that he knows in history outside the gates of paradise with the way barred against its return. We would misunderstand him and make of him a pessimist rather than a man of faith if we took this to mean that never, never could man hope to recover what was lost. The testimony of the prophets and the whole of Israel's eschatology tells us that faith in a sovereign God created ever-fresh visions of a final restoration of man. But these glowing hopes for the future never took the form of an unrealistic utopianism because the Israelite man of faith had his eyes opened to see realistically what it was in man that had lost him paradise and had to be overcome in him before he could return. He knew that the stream of history in which man finds himself flows not through paradise but through a broken world outside the gates of paradise.

Utopianism is a constant temptation particularly for people who have been exposed to the Scriptures, and there is a danger that our teaching of the Scriptures may encourage utopian development in our pupils. Utopianism consists essentially of an intensification of the prophetic vision of a world in which truth and justice and purity prevail but without the prophetic consciousness of the stubborn and deep-rooted forces in the human self, in *all* our human selves, which prevent the realization of that world today and tomorrow. There are widely varying forms of utopianism. There is a political form of it — the belief that, if only we could hit upon the right type of political and economic organization, we could reach paradise tomorrow. There are some in our midst who are convinced that democratic institutions are not just the most effective in safeguarding human liberties and in advancing human welfare, but also that if they were universally adopted, they would inaugurate a golden age. But on the other side of the fence are the communists, who are equally sure that their form of government and their organization of society must eventually establish a paradise on earth. The miscalculation of both groups lies in their blindness to the depth of the human problem. They are certain that man, by his cunning, has devised an instrument, a system, by which he can force open the gates of paradise without the humiliation or the personal ordeal of having to face and grapple with an essential wrongness not just in his institutions but in himself.

There is another form of utopianism that has disastrous consequences for marriage and the home. Young people are encouraged in the idea that when two persons who are really meant for each other meet and fall in love, this should be for them their passkey to paradise. And the bliss they experience in their love confirms them in this expectation. Their peril, then, lies in their awakening to the reality of their human situation as two human beings, each of whom has a natural capacity to make life not heaven but hell for the other. If they do not know what the ancient Hebrew writer knew, that this is the reality of every human situation in which two or more people are involved, and that marriage is likely to be something less than paradise as long as the pride of self in man remains unconquered, then that awakening may be interpreted by one or both of them as the discovery that they were not really meant for each other. Every human marriage participates in the brokenness of the world and of the humanity of which it is a part. It is entered upon and has to be lived out in the region outside the gates of paradise and yet with the hope and promise that insofar as human love becomes a reflection of God's own love, marriage and the home can be a foretaste of paradise restored.

There is yet another utopianism that has its locale in the church. Frequently it makes young people, and not only young people, impatient at the discrepancy between the life of the church as they experience it and the life of the true church as they conceive it. They form in their minds the image of a church that is perfectly faithful to its confession, free of all pettiness and selfishness, bold in its stand against all injustice and prejudice, a fellowship in which each is open to share with the other. What they actually have in mind is a church that has reached its goal and whose members have all been transformed into the likeness of their Master. They do well to reach out impatiently toward this church and to rebel against everything in the existing church that stands in contradiction to it. But to expect a utopian church today or tomorrow is to betray a most unchristian blindness to the forces not just in others but in ourselves that make the church the broken and imperfect society that it is. The church too has to live its life in a world outside the gates of paradise.

THE MYSTERY OF MAN

We must look more carefully now at this man who lost his Eden, but never for one moment should we lose the consciousness that the man who is being described for us is ourselves. If we know how deep is the mystery of the human self, we shall be the more ready to hear what is said. There is a widespread illusion that, while God is a mystery to man, man himself is no mystery. Especially in our modern world where psychology and psychiatry have delved into the human consciousness, the confidence has grown that man has definite and solid knowledge of himself. How could man be a mystery when there are so many specimens available for investigation and each man has only to turn his eyes inward to behold himself? But the fact is that the man who turns his eyes inward may fail entirely to see himself and that self-knowledge even with the aid of psychology and psychiatry is most difficult of attainment. Why is it that man, who can by his science achieve such masterly knowledge in so many spheres, fails so miserably when it comes to knowing man? The source of the most tragic confusion both in the lives of individuals and in society lies at this point, that men do not know who they are. Some tell themselves that they are only clever animals and others at the opposite extreme reassure themselves that they are somehow divine. Between these two extremes are an infinite series of variations. The Greeks for whom mind was divine and matter evil conceived man as a divine mind imprisoned in a body. Rousseau decreed that man was by nature good, all the evils and perversions of his life proceeding from his institutions. Some forms of Christianity have held that man is by nature evil, wholly evil, until by his conversion he is transformed into a child of God.

The answer to the question, Who is man? or more personally, Who am I? is never a rational deduction from the phenomena of life. A number of answers are possible, and each one belongs in the context of a total approach to the world and life. Each is at root an assertion of faith concerning the nature and meaning of life itself. None can be proved or disproved, because the self of man, like the reality of God, belongs to the realm of the unseen. The psychiatrist Rudolf Allers acknowledges that when he and his colleagues come up against the ultimate question of the nature of man, they are in a region into which their investigations are unable to penetrate and they have to turn to the philosophers for an answer. The Christian theologian, however, would have to say that the mystery extends beyond the reach of the philosopher. Since the most basic and decisive aspect of man's life is his relation with God, and because he cannot know himself apart from this relation, the question is in its deepest root theological, and the mystery of man's nature is analagous to the mystery of God's nature. Theology and anthropology are inseparable. God and man are so bound together that there can be no knowledge of the one without knowledge of the other.

Let us take the simple statement of our author, then, that God made man of the dust of the earth, breathing into him the breath of life so that he became a living soul. At first sight this seems a naïve conception of a human body, formed of earth and brought alive by God breathing into it his own breath. But in the larger context of Old Testament faith it expresses the completeness of man's dependence upon God for life. God sends forth his breath and man lives; he takes it again and man dies. Man lives in constant dependence upon that which comes forth from the mouth of God. From God's mouth come promises that must be grasped and commands that must be obeyed if the life-giving relation between man and God is to be sustained. One of the functions of God's word is to draw a line beyond which man cannot pass, and if he dares to pass, he brings upon himself his own destruction. Man's nature begins to be defined thus in relation to God. He is a creature whose very life is God's gift to him. His uniqueness is the freedom with which he is able to hear and to respond to God's commands. The only limitation on his freedom is where his will might come in conflict with the will of God. God entrusts to him the care of the garden, but requires of him that he hold himself within certain bounds.

What interests us most, however, in the description of man is that he is a " living soul " or a " living self." He is not a soul implanted in a body, but rather, his body might be said to be an integral aspect of his soul or self. The Hebrews did not make a clear distinction between the intangible and the tangible elements in man. " All flesh " is an adequate description of all mankind. Whatever aspect of man's being is referred to, it signifies the whole man. To present one's body to be a living sacrifice is to present one's self. When Jesus gives his body to his disciples in the bread and wine of the Last Supper he points them to his giving of himself to them. It is not an accident that this understanding of man arose in the context of a theology that was dominated by faith in one sovereign God. The unity of God calls for a unity in the nature of the man who is created for fellowship with God. In the ancient world the worship of multiple gods meant the organization of man's existence around multiple centers. Divided in his loyalties, he was divided in himself. The wholeness of his nature could be realized only when his entire existence was unified in the love and worship of one God. Because it was the nature of God to claim all things in the creation, both material and spiritual, as his own, the man who responded to this claim was one in body, mind, and spirit. God's relation was not with some one part, a religious or spiritual part, of his existence, but with his whole self.

This definition of man has far-reaching consequences. It exposes the falsity of the distinction between the spiritual and the material where God's relation with man is concerned. The supposition that Christianity is concerned only with spiritual things, that the gospel has to do only with the inner life of man, makes a false and unreal division in man. God's concern is with the whole man, the inner man, the economic man, the social man, the recreational man, the political man. To some, it used to sound pious for churchmen to say that they cared only for the souls of men, but where are the souls of men so clearly exposed as in the marketplace and the polling booth and the open street?

THE SOCIAL INVOLVEMENT OF MAN

The next stage in the definition of humanity is that it consists of man and woman. It is not good for either of them to be alone. Each is incomplete without the other. We begin here to see that man was not made to have his existence in himself alone. Rather, he was fashioned for a double dependency: to have his life first in a relationship with God and second in relationship with another human being, alongside him, like him and yet unlike him. These two relationships have remarkable similarities. It is no accident that in both the Old and the New Testament the relation of God's people to their God is likened to the relation between man and wife. God is Israel's husband. The church is the bride of Christ. A man shall forsake his father and mother and cleave to his wife so that they become one flesh, that is, one self, a unity in which both find their freedom and their fulfillment. The relationship of marriage claims each member to it totally, and the completeness of the unity depends upon the measure in which they surrender to that claim. But so is it also in man's relationship with God. It is an unconditional relationship. It does not tolerate any division or limitation within it. God's giving of himself to man demands a response in which man loves God with all his mind and heart and soul and strength.

Here the Biblical mind comes most sharply into conflict with the modern mind. We tend to start from man as an autonomous being and to consider only on a secondary level the possibility of his relationships with God and other human beings. We think of him first as existing as an individual and then as entering into relationship with other existences. But in Scripture, man as an individual cut off from God and his fellowman is cut off from life itself. He exists from the beginning in relationships with God and with the person alongside him, so that to assert his own self-sovereignty he has to disrupt both relationships. He cannot escape either from God or from his neighbor. He has no means of walling himself in so that he is by himself alone. When he attempts it, he merely turns the relationships that have in them the promise and possibility of life into instruments of death and destruction.

The third chapter of Genesis is a representation of how and why man, created for a life of blessedness in this double relationship with God and with his human partner, nevertheless took the wrong turn and missed his destiny. It is a marvelously accurate picture of how evil finds its way into human life. The trouble begins with a questioning of God's commands. The voice of the serpent asks whether the limitation on man's freedom, the line that God has drawn, should be taken quite so seriously as it is. There are fruits on the other side of the line that would be most delightful to have. Why let even a commandment of God restrain you? But the ultimate temptation to humanity lay in the suggestion: Do what you like in this instance and you will discover that you yourselves are like gods. Here the ancient writer, like a true physician, lays his finger on the source of the poison that has perverted human life through the ages. Man is betrayed by his impatience with even a single restraint upon his freedom, by his desire for complete and unlimited autonomy, by an urge within his ego to be like a god himself rather than to be under the authority of God. He does not want to be bound, but he does not know that his choice in actuality is whether to be bound and limited by an authority beyond himself in a relationship of trust and love or to be in rebellion against inescapable bonds in an atmosphere of guilt and fear.

This picture of the origin of evil does two things. It prevents any suggestion that evil is intrinsic to the nature of the creation, so that man is merely its victim, by tracing its origin to man's misuse of his God-given freedom. The responsibility is placed squarely upon man's decision. Yet at the same time it takes account of the subtle and insidious character of evil as something that attacks man from without and lures him to his destruction. Man is open on the one side to the voice of God, but from the other side a voice sounds in his ears that mocks and questions the truth of what God has said and incites him to rebellion. The picture in Jesus' parable of the prodigal is simpler and yet it is essentially the same. The son is dissatisfied under the authority of the father. He wants the freedom to rule his own life and possessions. He goes into the far country in order to cut himself apart from the restraining relation with the father. But soon he discovers that self-sovereignty has led him to the verge of self-destruction.

Anyone who undertakes to develop this theme, on either its Old Testament or its New Testament basis, will do well to take account of the wide popularity today of a philosophy of self-fulfillment through self-sovereignty. In its various forms it is like sugar to the human ego. It tells man what he wants to hear. He was born to be a king. His life is his own to do with it what he will. Freedom is his God-given heritage, freedom to determine all things in his individual existence without let or hindrance from any quarter. There are wide variations in how this is interpreted. A John Birch Society member regards the levying of income taxes as an infringement of his individual self-sovereignty. But at the opposite pole are highly intelligent people who recognize that compromises must be made if society is to exist at all, the freedom of one man being limited by the legitimate interests of another, and yet whose basic philosophy of life has at its core an affirmation of the natural drive of the human self toward sovereignty. The Greeks were neither the first nor the last to hold that civilization rests on a basis of intelligent self-interest. Their man-centered order of life, which has to such a degree shaped our modern world, proceeded from the assumption that self-centeredness is not only the reasonable order but actually the only possible order of life. From this standpoint it seemed to them ridiculous and irrational for the Christian gospel to demand the abdication of sovereignty by the human self and the unconditional surrender of the central ruling place in life to God.

Genesis, ch. 3, prepares the way for the totalitarian claim upon the human self that is ultimately to be made by Jesus Christ. The cross of Jesus Christ unmasks in good men, highly civilized men, earnestly religious men, a self that, when it is confronted nakedly with God's unconditional claim, defends its self-sovereignty jealously, and in hatred of him in whom the claim is made sends him to his death. The Old Testament prophet, because he already knew the presence of the God who was to be revealed in Jesus Christ, was already conscious of what it was in man that disrupted his relation with God and brought disorder and ruin into human life: the lust for absolute and unconditional freedom, the drive to self-sovereignty, the unwillingness to be a creature limited and fulfilled by God's command.

There is one final point at which this portrait of man contradicts modern man's portrait of himself. Adam and Eve, following their act of disobedience, are represented as hiding from God, fearing his approach, fleeing from his presence. Openness and trust have been replaced by guilt and fear. But this is not how man today usually pictures himself in relation to God. He tells himself that he is in search of God. God is a problem to him, an important problem into which he must delve earnestly, a source of perplexity and confusion. He must think and think and think until he finds some satisfactory answer to the question of God. But Genesis says to us that it is not God who is the problem but man. And far from being in search of God, man is constantly in flight from God because of his desperate fear of having the whole truth about himself laid bare. He wants to conceal not only the resistance of his inmost self to God but also the humiliation into which this resistance has brought him, and even in the midst of his secret humiliation he wants to protect his own self-sovereignty against the approach of God. The truth is not that he is seeking God but that God is seeking him, putting questions to him that he does not wish to answer: " Where art thou? " " What hast thou done? " and we may add here God's question to Cain in ch. 4: "Where is thy brother?" No man can escape from these questions which God puts to him. They are lodged like arrows in his being. They are questions that remind him that he does not exist alone, that he exists in relationships, with God and with the person alongside him, which make him a responsible being.

It is significant that both Adam and Eve attempt to evade the responsibility for their action, Adam asserting his innocence and laying the blame on Eve, and Eve in turn laying the blame on the serpent. The attempt to place the responsibility somewhere else than within oneself is just one aspect of the evasion of God. All flight from responsibility is at root flight from God. Yet such flight is futile because the relationships that make us responsible remain. It is not in our power to dissolve them, but only to disrupt them, and such relationships in their disruption take on the character of a curse. God's claim upon man's life that is experienced as love by the man who is open to be claimed by God becomes the very anger of an enemy and a deadly threat to his existence for the man who is estranged from God. But perhaps if man in estrangement looks into such a passage as Gen., ch. 3, as into a mirror, and catches a glimpse of himself in flight, he may suddenly come to himself, and giving up all thought of self-concealment, be willing to stand exposed before God as the wayward creature that he is.

Here, then, is where Genesis leaves us, and someone may ask whether it really performs a *Christian* office if it does no more. We can say on the highest authority that it does. None other than Jesus himself pictured a man standing, certainly outside the gates of paradise, beating upon his breast and crying, "God, be merciful to me a sinner," and said of him, "This man went down to his house justified." We do not have to insert the name of Jesus Christ into the third chapter of Genesis in order to make it Christian. We have only to let it strip us of our pretentions and set us where we belong before God and in the midst of our fellowmen, and when we come into that place of humiliation we shall find Jesus Christ awaiting us there that he may send us down to our house justified.

IV

THE SACRIFICE OF ISAAC

THERE ARE FEW STORIES in the Old Testament that are more alien and offensive to the mind of modern man than that of the sacrifice of Isaac. The succession of pictures that it conjures up makes us wonder why such a story was preserved in Holy Scripture: the command of God (even though intended only as a test of faith) that Abraham should kill the son of his old age, his only son, as a sacrifice; the seeming heartlessness of Abraham as he proceeds methodically to obey the command instead of defying it in the name of simple humanity and a father's love for his child; the boy climbing the mountainside with the wood on his back for the fire that was intended to char his body; the boy bound and lying on the wood with the knife in his father's hand poised above him. And perhaps the picture from which we recoil most is that of God letting Abraham carry the whole ghastly affair through to the next to the last moment before putting a stop to it. Did God really need to let it go so far in order to know how faithful Abraham would be to him? David Daiches, whose father was for many years the chief rabbi of Edinburgh, tells in his autobiography how in his boyhood this story terrified him. He hated it, and it seemed to him not a God but a devil who would demand that a man sacrifice his son to him. What hope is there that God should really speak to modern man through the medium of such an ancient story?

We have first to ask why it was preserved by the Hebrews. One explanation may be that it was recognized as such a superb example of the storyteller's art that the sheer fascination of it was sufficient to account for its survival. The simplicity with which the tale unfolds with steadily mounting tension until the climax is reached still impresses us today, and we can imagine the force of it when it was told by word of mouth to people in whose world human sacrifice was not unknown. The setting is important. Abraham has been given the promise of a great future, but the fulfillment of God's promise has seemed impossible because of his and Sarah's childlessness. Then comes the miracle of Isaac's birth, and all of Abraham's hopes are set upon this son. Only against this background do we see the full force of the incomprehensibility of God's command to sacrifice Isaac. Abraham is being commanded to destroy the one human possibility of that great future which God has promised him. We see Abraham in the early morning cutting the wood for the fire and making ready for the journey, telling his son only that they have a sacrifice to make. We see him with his donkey, two servants, and his son plodding on for three days, weighed down with the terror of what he must do in obedience to God. The tension mounts as father and son leave the servants and the donkey and go the last stage of the journey alone, Isaac carrying the wood on his back and Abraham with the fire in one hand and the knife in the other. As they go, Isaac asks his innocent question: " Father, here is wood and fire, but where is the lamb for the burnt offering? " And Abraham returns his evasive answer: " God will provide a lamb for the burnt offering." They come to the top of the mountain; the wood is laid ready and the child is stretched upon it. But with his hand raised to strike the death blow, Abraham hears the new command, the word of release: " Do the child no harm," and a lamb caught in a nearby thicket provides a substitute sacrifice. With what excitement would each generation of Israelites listen to that story!

A second suggestion that has received attention is that the story has a cultic context, that it was told at one of the Palestinian shrines to explain why for Israelites a lamb was regarded as an acceptable sacrifice, where in earlier practice the firstborn son had been claimed by the god of the shrine. We are reminded that in the nations surrounding Israel the practice of human sacrifice was known and that in times of severe crisis the Israelites themselves resorted to it in the hope that such an offering would placate the anger of their god. That may be an interesting speculation concerning an earlier form of the tradition than we have here and as such may have some truth in it, but it throws no light on the present form of the tradition where it is no longer a story told at a local shrine, but is embedded in a prophetic narrative concerning the origins of Israel's life and destiny. The question has to be faced: Why would men who were imbued with the prophetic spirit and in whose teachings human sacrifice had long ago been condemned as a pagan practice, utterly abhorrent to their God, nevertheless represent the ancestor of their faith as proceeding in obedience to God to perform such a practice? We cannot be content to think that they preserved the story merely because of its literary merit or as an explanation of how human sacrifice came to be so decisively abandoned by the Israelites.

The Representative Character of Abraham

We need to go back a step and ask some questions concerning the significance of all the Abraham stories in the life of Israel. Gerhard von Rad has taught us to see in Deut. 26:5 f. a very early Israelite confession of faith. I suggest that you watch what becomes of the figure of the patriarch in it, whether he be Abraham or Jacob: " A wandering Aramaean was my father; and he went down into Egypt and sojourned there, few in number; and there he became a nation, great, mighty, and populous. And the Egyptians treated us harshly and afflicted us. . . ." Do you see what happens to Abraham in this confession? Beginning as one man, a wandering Aramaean, he has quickly come to represent the whole family that went down to Egypt, then a nation, and finally he is identified with the confessor himself. Abraham, the ancestor of Israel, has ceased to be merely an individual in the distant past and has become the incorporation of the destiny of his posterity. We see this happening with other figures in the patriarchal stories. Jacob and Esau represent the nations of Israel and Edom, and the rivalry of the brothers, beginning while they were still in the womb of their mother, mirrors the agelong rivalry of these Palestinian neighbors. Something also of the character of the two nations was depicted in the character of their ancestors. In a similar way Abraham is made the bearer of Israel's consciousness of high destiny. God's choice of Abraham to be the special instrument of his redemptive purpose in the world is God's choice of Israel. The command to Abraham to leave his homeland and his kindred and to become a wanderer on earth in God's service defines the destiny of Israel. The promise of blessing for all the families of the earth through Abraham is intended definitely in Gen. 12:1-4 to be read as a promise to the descendants of Abraham. It is not just the one man Abraham but all who have come forth from Abraham who are singled out to represent God in such a way that he who blesses them is blessed and he who curses them is cursed.

Does this mean, then, that Abraham is to be explained simply as a projection of Israel's self-consciousness upon the screen of patriarchal times? If we were to leave that impression, we would do a serious injustice to the facts. The work of Albrecht Alt and W. F. Albright has led to a much higher estimate of the historical content of the stories of the patriarchs than was usual in the nineteenth century. Alt, with his theory of how the stories of Abraham, Isaac, and Jacob were preserved at the shrines of Hebron, Beer-sheba, and Shechem, and his demonstration of how such cultic traditions could retain for centuries a genuine folk memory of original events and persons, has made it possible to claim a solid historical nucleus for the stories. Albright has made his contribution from archaeology by showing that some of the patriarchal traditions have features that correspond to the cultural characteristics of that early age as they have been established archaeologically and do not fit nearly so well in the much later times from which they have been supposed to have come. Such findings as these must not be made the basis for extravagant assumptions about the historicity of the stories. The most we can say is that traditions which embody a genuine memory of Israel's ancestors have become through the years the vehicle of the nation's consciousness not only of its destiny but also of its temptations, not only of the unique relation of Israel with God but also of the unique trials and desperate situations into which that relationship brought the nation.

We have an excellent example in the New Testament in Heb. 11:8-10 of how Abraham became for later ages an embodiment of what it means in any age to be a man of faith. " By faith Abraham obeyed when he was called to go out to a place which he was to receive as an inheritance; and he went out, not knowing where he was to go. By faith he sojourned in the land of promise, as in a foreign land. . . . For he looked forward to the city which has foundations, whose builder and maker is God." That is a Christian interpretation of Abraham. Clearly you can see the figure of the patriarch of Genesis, but, without distorting the figure, the author of Hebrews has fashioned him into a bearer of the Christian hope, the pilgrim who at the call of God leaves behind the ordinary securities of life and is not ever again quite at home even in his homeland because he is haunted by the vision of the city of God, a realm of truth and mercy and brotherhood that God has ordained as the goal of human life. The man of faith is led on by the vision, never quite certain where it will take him next. Already in Genesis this process is far advanced by which Abraham became a figure in whom every Israelite was intended to see something of his destiny in the sight of God. As long as these stories were told, Abraham was not dead, but was to each new age a representation of all that was involved in being a people chosen of God to be the human instrument of His redemptive purpose for the world. But this identification of the believer with Abraham was not confined to Israel. The Christians of the early church, claiming to be the New Israel of God and the true continuation of the redemptive history that reached its climax in the Israelite, Jesus Christ, saw in Abraham their own ancestor in the faith and interpreted the stories of

Abraham as revelations of the destiny that was now being fulfilled in themselves.

OUR INVOLVEMENT IN ABRAHAM'S ELECTION

The first stage, then, in the dialogue of modern man with any
story of Abraham is for him to discover his own involvement in
Abraham. What appears at first to be just a curious, ancient
Aramaean moving across the horizon of patriarchal times and
having strange things happen to him has to be recognized as a
representation of what it means for any one of us to be singled
out by God to be the bearer of his purpose. But it is directly here
that modern man has his greatest difficulty with Abraham. All
this talk about God's choosing Abraham to stand in a special relation with himself, calling him, promising him a unique destiny
on behalf of his fellowmen, leaves modern man cold. This seems
to him to be just one form of that egotistical idea with which
Israel was obsessed, which has made it hold itself apart from other
peoples through all its history and earned it their antagonism and
resentment, the idea that they are a chosen people, related to God
as no other people is. The election of Abraham is the stumbling
block. How can God be said to fasten his concern upon one man
or one nation without compromising the truth of his loving concern for all men? And how can any man regard himself as the
elect one of God without being betrayed into a fatal self-righteous-
ness and into insidious pretentions of superiority? Add to this
the fact that in the ancient Near East there were numerous examples of nations that claimed for themselves a specially privileged position in relation to the god whom they worshiped. Also,
in the modern world we have had some unsavory examples of
nations that regarded themselves as the chosen people of God.

To see the Biblical doctrine of election in this context, however, is to misunderstand it completely. There is no contradiction
between it and the universality of God's concern for mankind.
On the contrary, it is made plain in the verses that tell of God's
choice of Abraham that he is chosen, not for his own sake or for
the sake of some one nation, but that all the families of the earth

may find blessedness. There are eleven chapters in Genesis that form the background of the call of Abraham. They portray a world that has lost its way, a world created to be a place of blessing where men and women will reflect in themselves and in their relations with one another the very nature of God himself, but a world in which life has been darkened and brought under a curse by man's rebellion against God issuing in the loss of his humanity. Genesis, ch. 12, depicts the first stage in the story of God's redemption of man. It begins with God laying his hand upon a man in Mesopotamia, singling him out, calling him in such a way that in obedience he has to go out into the unknown to have a new life shaped for him in relation with the God who has called him. But it very soon becomes plain that he has not been given any specially privileged position with God; rather, he has less security than other men, greater sacrifices to make, greater trials to endure. His relation with God makes life not easier but much more difficult for him. And never is he encouraged to think that he is better than anybody else.

Abraham is just the first of a long succession of men who knew themselves chosen of God. You might say that the God of Israel can be defined as the God who chooses the men he needs for his service. Prophets such as Amos, Isaiah, and Jeremiah let you look directly into the experiences in which they became aware of the hand of God being laid upon them. There is no temptation for any of them to give themselves airs because of the intimate and unique relation with God into which this brings them, because they know only too well the terrifying responsibility that the relation lays upon them. Some Israelites might misinterpret their chosenness, taking it as a mark of moral and spiritual superiority and the basis for claiming a privileged position with God, but there was usually a prophet such as Amos to remind them that the knowledge of God conferred not special privileges but special responsibilities. Second Isaiah's " servant Israel " clarifies once and for all the place of a special people of God in the unfolding of God's purpose for the whole world. God's word not only reveals his purpose but exerts its creative power in the life of man, and has to be lodged in a people who will let their life become a witness to this word and will offer themselves for the service of this word, no matter how great the cost. The faithful servant has to be ready even to die in the performance of his task, but in his death he bears his witness and light shines forth to the ends of the earth to lighten the nations.

The Biblical doctrine of election comes to its focus in Jesus Christ. There is a real sense in which we understand neither Abraham's chosenness nor our own until we know something of what it meant for Jesus to be the chosen one of God. Whether we interpret the story of Jesus' baptism as a construct of the church or as an account of a visionary experience in which he became conscious of his destiny (the latter is my preference, but both must be recognized as possibilities), it speaks plainly of the unique relation in which Jesus stood with the Father: "Thou art my beloved Son in whom I am well pleased." His chosenness in which he is singled out from all humanity for a relation with God that no other human being had ever known lays upon him the colossal and fearful burden of standing in the gap between a holy and loving God and a sinful and rebellious humanity. To have to go his way alone as the bearer of God's cause and God's purpose for all mankind, to have as the root and substance of his every word and action the word of God that is at one and the same time God's promise of life and his sentence of death upon men, that was the meaning of election for Jesus Christ. But it was not for him alone, because he reached out and chose for himself disciples and through those disciples a church, an ecclesia, the fellowship of those who knew themselves called and marked out to share with him both his relation with God and his service of God.

To be truly in the church of Jesus Christ is therefore to find oneself standing in this succession of the "elect." The word "elect" suffered a serious and unbiblical perversion when during the sixteenth and seventeenth centuries it was used to designate a portion of mankind whose salvation had been determined by God from the beginning, while all the remainder of mankind was declared "reprobate," with no possibility of salvation. In contrast to that, the "elect" in Scripture, whether it be Abraham or Jeremiah or Israel or Jesus Christ or the church, is always chosen for the sake of a reprobate humanity, a lost and broken world. To belong in the number of the "elect" means to have responded to the call of God, "Whom shall I send and who will go for us?" and so to have offered oneself as the human agency that God needs in order to redeem a lost world. There is an unbroken line, then, that runs from Abraham through Israel to Jesus Christ and from Jesus Christ through his apostles to everyone who knows himself called of God into membership in the body of Christ. We are not strangers to Abraham, nor is he a stranger to us though thousands of years and vast differences may seem to separate us. We are of one company, sharing in the same calling and destiny.

THE TESTING OF ABRAHAM

At last we come back now to the story of Abraham and Isaac. Genesis, ch. 21, narrated the birth of Isaac. The emphasis upon the great age of Sarah and Abraham when their son was born develops a familiar Old Testament theme — that through faith in God the seemingly impossible becomes not only possible but actual. Israel was conscious that its very existence as a nation was the product of a kind of continuous miracle. It looked back to its origin in the exodus when a band of disorganized slaves had in one generation become a nation with a destiny, and saw in the whole of it the accomplishment of the impossible. It was a gigantic miracle. Time after time the obstacles were insuperable and there seemed to be no way through, but faith moved mountains and a way appeared. The very beginning of the world was conceived on the same pattern, a creation out of nothing, a conquest of chaos. So also with Abraham: the promise of a great future seemed impossible of fulfillment as the years wore on, since Abraham and Sarah had no child. But the God who made the promise opened the way for its fulfillment when unexpectedly he gave them a son, Isaac. Isaac was Abraham's hope. But God's greatest gifts can constitute a man's most subtle temptation to unfaithfulness. Isaac, who was God's gift of a future to Abraham, could so easily become more dear to Abraham than God himself. But this was what God could not permit to happen with Abraham, for, if Abraham let even his beloved child begin to take the place in his heart that belonged to God alone, then he would have ceased to be the father of the covenant people of God. Abraham is the Abraham whom God has called and chosen only if he belongs unconditionally to God. Therefore God put Abraham to the test in order that the purity and wholeness of Abraham's faith and obedience might shine forth in their full glory.

We hear elsewhere in Scripture of God's testing men of faith. There is the testing of Job, when Satan is permitted to strip from him all his possessions and his children and to leave him desolate upon an ash heap, a mass of boils, hating his life, that the integrity of his faith might appear. There is the testing of Jeremiah, when in the bitterness of his sufferings he reproached God with breaking his promise to him and threatened to be silent in the future, yet found at the critical moment that he was bound to God in such an unconditional way that he could not restrain God's word when it needed to be spoken. Then there is the testing of our Lord himself. He was not ready for his ministry until the consciousness of his unique destiny that came to him at his baptism had been tested and thereby clarified in the wilderness. God's testing of the man of his choice is an important element in his dealings with him. Whoever hears and responds to God's call can expect to be tested. It is a confrontation with alternatives that makes it necessary for a man to demonstrate both to God and to himself the nature of his relationship with God. The rich young ruler faced just such a test when Jesus, " looking on him, loved him " and desired to make him a disciple, but first set him in a situation that would reveal where God really stood in this deeply moral and religious man's life. The young man failed the test because the hidden and unsuspected reality was that his possessions were dearer to him than his God.

All these tests say the same thing about the relation of God with the man who is chosen to be the bearer of his purpose among men. The covenant bond between God and the man of his choice has to be unconditional. The reason that in the Old Testament, and in the New as well, the term " servant " or " slave " is used so frequently, not only for Israel and for many of the greatest figures in the history of Israel but also for Jesus and his apostles, is that it expresses the consciousness of the man of faith that he is totally at the disposal of God. The slave was the property of his master. We need to remember also that the same term was used for the prime minister of the king who was most in the king's confidence. Israel the servant was bound absolutely to the will of God and yet in being bound became the " man of God's counsel " and the instrument of his purpose. The power of faith lay in this unconditional and unobstructed openness to God. Let anything come between to capture and deflect the allegiance of man's being so that his life has its center and focus only partly in God, and his power is gone. In the light of this we understand the severity of Jesus' totalitarian claim upon the human self. " If any one comes to me and does not hate his own father and mother and wife and children and brothers and sisters, yes, and even his own life, he cannot be my disciple." It is unreasonable, highly unreasonable. It asks of a man more than the human self finds it practicable to give. Therefore we customarily soft-pedal such passages as these in our preaching and teaching for fear the very unreasonableness of such demands may frighten people away from the Christian faith. And then we wonder why the faith of those whom we capture by these means has in it no power to move mountains. No power is promised anywhere in Scripture to people with a reasonable, moderate faith. The faith that has power in it is the faith of an Abraham or of a Job or of a Jeremiah who has let himself be bound so unconditionally to God that his whole existence is in God's hand as a ready instrument for the fulfillment of his purpose. God cannot get hold of a man who belongs only 60 or 80 or 90 percent to him. A reservation in our relation means that we have left ourselves a way of escape from God, that we have reserved for ourselves the freedom to say no to God if the cost of faith should become too steep. The glory of Abraham in the memory of Israel was that, even when the cost of unconditional obedience was the sacrifice of his own son, and with his son, of his own future, he did not waver for a moment in his faith. To us as Christians, that is a foreshadowing of the perfect obedience of Jesus Christ whose will was so completely at one with the will of God that for him there could be no turning aside when the clash of God's will in him with the will of man set the horror of the cross at the end of the road. Abraham's hand was stayed and a substitute was found in the thicket, but when this greater sacrifice was demanded, there was no staying of the hand of the executioner and no substitute appeared at the last moment.

Our God is a jealous God. He will not share the worship of our hearts with anyone or with anything; it must be concentrated upon him alone. For that reason Jesus and the apostles insisted that there was no way to man's true fulfillment of his life except by way of a death to self. Unfortunately when Jesus says, " You must die to live " men often hear only the first three words, " You must die," as though an inhuman sacrifice were being demanded of them, when in actuality Jesus is disclosing to them the secret of how they may be joyfully and triumphantly alive in God. It is love that speaks when he claims this sacrifice. He is saying: " Let God be God for you, the truly sovereign God in your existence, if you would know the wholeness of your life in God." When we conceal this uncompromising claim and offer the gifts of God — the good life, forgiveness, peace with God, spiritual security — at a lesser price, we make of our church a kind of bargain counter of salvation. We let family, nation, and all manner of importunate personal interests take the primary place in men's lives and are content so long as they are willing to give God a place even though it may be a subordinate one, unaware that we have betrayed our people into a fatal disorder. God will not take second place. He withholds himself and the blessings of his presence from us until we are willing to accord him the honor and the undivided worship that are his due.

Faith as Obedience

A second point at which the story of Abraham's sacrifice of Isaac may speak sharply to modern man is in its definition of the content of faith as a resolute step-by-step obedience to God's commands. We are more likely today to talk of our ideals than of God's commands. The terms " command " and " obedience " are not popular among us. We like to think we are asserting our wills in freedom rather than that we are bowing our wills in obedience. It is slaves who obey; free men choose for themselves what they are to do in the light of their ideals. But ideals have in them a pliability, a capacity for being shaped in accord with the aspirations of men, while divine commands leave men only the alternatives of yes and no. One is able to feel a certain virtuousness just from the cherishing of ideals, even though the conduct of life may be far from their realization. They leave one with only a consciousness of imperfection, while God's commands fasten upon one the guilt of rebellion and disobedience. In ideals a man essentially is not carried beyond himself and his society, but when the commandments come upon the scene he knows that he has to do with God.

An unconditional faith in God receives its content from the nature of God himself. To enter into an intimate personal relation with him is to know him in his holiness, love, truth, justice, mercy, which at once discloses to the worshiper his own unholiness, lovelessness, falsity, injustice, and hardness of heart. God's commands are simply the demands of his nature upon those who would live in covenant fellowship with him: that they should reflect in their natures his very likeness. A merciful God cannot keep company with unmerciful men. The holiness of his nature calls for holiness in his people. His justice must be reflected in their dealings with one another. Therefore faith in him is inconceivable without an obedient response to the claims of his nature upon the believer. Disobedience to his commands denotes not just an imperfection in the relationship, but rather the rupture of it and the replacement of trust by a rebellion of the human will. The obedience of Abraham therefore discloses a consciousness in Israel of the radical claim that God makes not just on the inner being but also on the outward conduct of the man whom he chooses to be the instrument of his purpose — obedience to his will step by step even though each step seems merely to take him that much closer to death. Already in Abraham there is a suggestion of the costliness of such obedience and a foreshadowing of what God would have to expect of one who would offer him a perfect obedience that in his obedience God's power might be perfectly revealed.

The lamb that at the opportune moment was caught by its horns in a nearby thicket and that Abraham recognized as God's provision of a substitute sacrifice was undoubtedly intended to explain why in Israel lambs were an acceptable offering on occasions when in neighboring nations men went much farther and offered their sons. But if Israel saw itself and its own destiny in Abraham and expressed in this story God's demand upon his people that they be ready to surrender all that was most precious to them in obedience to him, then the lamb suggests that even when the way of obedience seems to be leading to death it may turn out to be the way to life and to a glorious future. God suddenly and to the surprise of his servant opens before him a totally new possibility where there had seemed to be nothing in prospect but death and despair. In fact, the way of obedience that seemed to lead to death was the narrow way that alone led into that glorious future. How many times in Israel must not only prophets such as Elijah and Amos and Jeremiah but whole communities of faithful believers have felt that the way of obedience to their God was none other than the certain road to death? What kept them faithful when there seemed humanly to be no prospect of survival for any who dared to be faithful? The miracle of Israel is that the light of faith kept burning in spite of all the forces that combined again and again to snuff it out. We may well believe that the story of Abraham's sacrifice played its part in that survival. Israelites, remembering that story in their lonely ordeal with death, would tell themselves that God was asking no more of them than he had asked of Abraham, and as they came to the climax of the story — God's provision that Isaac should not die but should become the father of a great people for the blessing of the earth — they would take fresh courage and believe that God would make a future where as yet their eyes could discern none.

V

ELIJAH ON MOUNT CARMEL

IN A DISCUSSION on "the Old Testament in dialogue with modern man," one might be expected to choose for consideration passages that by the nature of their content are likely to be most meaningful and relevant in the situations of our modern world. There are many such passages. Samuel's warning to Israel that the concentration of political power in a monarchy may lead to tyranny and to the loss by Israelites of many of the freedoms and privileges that have been distinctive of their nation can be applied almost directly to a world in which governmental power in many nations has become so colossal that it threateningly overshadows the life of the individual citizen. Amos' attack on the dishonesty of merchants who use false weights and cheat the poor out of a few ounces of every pound of food they buy is directly pertinent to the life of cities where butchers are found using dishonest scales, most of them usually in the poorer sections of the city. The Fifty-first Psalm can be read by a modern congregation as its confession of sin and plea for God's pardon without any consciousness that the author of that prayer is separated from them by some thousands of years and by vast differences in his cultural situation. We rarely think of how striking it is that so much in the Old Testament is immediately comprehensible and relevant to twentieth-century people. These are ancient Hebrew documents, composed at some time during the thousand years before the time of Jesus Christ, the products of a world that in many respects is completely alien to us, and yet men and women

with little education are able to read much of them with understanding and profit. Put in their hands a similar volume of ancient Greek literature or ancient Egyptian literature or ancient
Babylonian literature and how much of it will have meaning and
relevance for them? The earthiness and the consistency with
which the Old Testament grapples with the questions and problems not just of Hebrew man but of man as man, universal man,
is distinctive of the faith of Israel and arises from the nature of
the God whom they worshiped.

Some justification should perhaps be offered, then, for choosing
to deal, not with one of these immediately relevant and comprehensible passages, but instead with a highly dramatic story
that in many of its features creates serious problems for the modern mind. It would be difficult to find a passage that offers more
problems than the story of Elijah's contest with the prophets of
Baal on Mt. Carmel. It is a tremendous story and the author unfolds it with consummate skill. It is told for a later generation
of faithful worshipers of Yahweh to let them know how at a
critical moment in the past, when it seemed as though the true
worship of Yahweh in Israel were to be blotted out, this one
prophet, Elijah, stood boldly in the breach and won a great victory over the prophets of Baal. In the background, suggested
rather than described, is the massacre of prophets of Yahweh at
the bidding of the queen of Israel, a Tyrian princess who was
intent upon stamping out the austere religion of Israel and sub-
stituting for it the more sensuous Baal cult. The king is represented as a man of uncertain mind, unwilling to cast off all
respect for his ancestral faith, yet also unwilling to stand in the
way of his aggressive wife. He follows her counsel, but when
Elijah calls for a contest between himself and the prophets of
Baal with representatives of all Israel looking on, the king ac-
cedes to the prophet's request.

Two sacrifices are to be made ready, each consisting of a bul-
lock laid on wood, and the God who sends fire from heaven
to consume the sacrifice is to be acknowledged by Israel as the
one true God. Elijah stakes everything on this one venture. The

contrast between the approach of the Baal prophets to their god, a wild orgy of dancing, shrieking, and bloodletting, and Elijah's approach to his God, a simple prayer, is graphic and impressive. Elijah's preliminary act of having a large quantity of water poured over his sacrifice accentuates the miracle that is to follow. Fire falls from heaven and consumes both the sacrifice and the water all around it. The people confess their faith in the God who has answered by fire and make a speedy though gruesome end to the prophets of Baal.

The story was most impressive to ancient Israelites whose constant temptation for centuries after the time of Elijah was to soften the austerities of prophetic religion by combining it in some measure with the more indulgent and popular practices of the Baal cult. Elijah's opening question, " How long will you go limping with two different opinions? " concerned them very directly, and his ridicule of the priests and prophets of Baal would certainly make many Israelites ashamed of having had anything to do with such a cult. That God sent fire from heaven in answer to Elijah's prayer would not surprise them, for in the traditions of their faith God had often intervened at critical moments in a decisive fashion in order to maintain his cause. Nor would they be offended at the conclusion of the story, the slaughter of the four hundred prophets of Baal, because death to them was the appropriate end of all such enemies of God.

But the difficulty is that this story is told in Christian churches and church schools with the expectation that it should be as directly meaningful and impressive today as it was, let us say, in Judah in the seventh century B.C. The underlying presupposition is that nothing has happened since then to make our hearing of the story any different from the hearing of it then. But much has happened to make it impossible to equate the two hearings of it. For one thing, Jesus Christ has been born, has had his ministry, has had something to say about how God wins his victory and about how God expects us to deal with his enemies, has in fact died for the sake of his bitterest enemies. Does that make no difference? Only too often there have been Christians in history for whom it has indeed made no difference in their hearing of the story of Elijah. They have interpreted its presence in the Holy Scriptures as placing the stamp of divine approval upon the final action of Elijah and therefore as a divinely authorized license to them to go out and slaughter those whom they considered to be the enemies of God. Here, then, is the first problem: How is a Christian who really hears and responds to the word of Jesus Christ to understand this story of Elijah? This raises sharply the much larger question of the relation of the Old Testament to the New.

Problems That a Christian Must Face

But let us begin at the beginning and take note of all the problems that arise for us here. We shall merely list them at this point and make no attempt to deal with them. Putting this one story in the context of the total narrative concerning the prophets Elijah and Elisha in I and II Kings, we note at once a striking difference between the depiction of these prophets and the self-depiction of the great writing prophets such as Amos, Isaiah, and Jeremiah. The latter are men who speak for God and whose power is entirely in the word they speak, but the former are men who wield supernatural power. The narrative of their ministries is full to overflowing with reports of miraculous events. Ravens feed Elijah regularly each morning and evening when he is in hiding. King Ahab is warned that the destructive drought is to end only when Elijah says it shall. Twice Elijah calls down fire from heaven to destroy companies of fifty soldiers sent by King Ahaziah to bring the prophet before him. We are forced therefore to ask how we should evaluate the element of the miraculous in general in these stories. Then there is the problem inherent in the fact that Elijah is represented as staking the future of Yahweh's good name in Israel (also his own repute as a true prophet of Yahweh) upon his sending fire from heaven to consume the sacrifice. What is this except the requiring of a sign from heaven if the people are to believe, a demand that Paul later said was only too characteristic of his fellow countrymen (I Cor.

1:22)? We cannot forget that it was Satan who suggested to Jesus that he should demonstrate his divine power by jumping off the pinnacle of the Temple and having angels support him so that he would not come to grief on the stones below, nor that Jesus answered the tempter, quoting from Deuteronomy, " You shall not put the Lord your God to the test." As Christians, can we be really happy about Elijah's putting God to the test? Closely connected with this is the question whether faith that has its source in an outward demonstration of supernatural power is true faith with the promise of an enduring future. In John's Gospel the faith that arises merely from seeing the miracles is a superficial faith with no promise in it; not until the word of God is heard and received is there a response to God that is worthy of the name " faith." If Jesus had miraculously descended from the cross at the bidding of those who cried, " Let him come down now from the cross, and we will believe in him," what would have been the quality of their faith? Finally, there is the problem already mentioned of Elijah's slaughter of his enemies.

Here, then, is a passage from which we cannot lightly make transfers of meaning to the modern scene, in fact, a passage which, uninterpreted, can lead the reader into dangerously unchristian conceptions concerning God's relationship and dealings with man. But for that very reason it is a singularly valuable passage for our present study since it brings into the open certain important features of the Old Testament's dialogue with modern man that we are inclined frequently to leave unconsidered and undiscussed.

INCOMPLETENESS OF OLD TESTAMENT WITHOUT NEW

The first thing that becomes plain to us here is that the Christian cannot leave Jesus Christ out of his dialogue with the Old Testament; that is, he cannot go directly to the Old Testament as though it were for him the medium of God's revelation completely apart from its fulfillment in Jesus Christ. Paul, in II Cor. 3:14, says that the Jews who have not yet come to know the fullness of God's spirit in and through Jesus Christ have a veil over their minds when they hear the Old Testament, but when they turn to Christ and receive his Spirit, the veil is removed. What God is saying to his people in the Old Testament is rightly understood only when the final act of his revelation and redemption in Jesus Christ has unveiled the true significance of what he has been doing from the beginning. It is a mistake therefore to think that the Old Testament can stand by itself in isolation from the New. It is like a body without a head. It is like the first four acts of a drama in which the significance of what is happening is not fully revealed until the fifth act. The Old Testament attains what is perhaps its highest point in Second Isaiah, and at that point it reaches out passionately toward a fulfillment that is yet to come. The movement of the Old Testament from the beginning is from promise to fulfillment, but always the fulfillment is incomplete and points forward to another fulfillment that lies beyond. The Creation presages a new creation, the exodus a new exodus, and the covenant a new covenant, but at the end of the Old Testament we are left waiting for this great new day to come. The claim of the New Testament is that in Jesus Christ the new day has come. With him began nothing less than a new creation in which he was a new Adam and his disciples new creatures by faith in him. By his life and death he effected the new exodus, the deliverance not just of Israel but of all mankind out of the slavery of a world of sin and death. In him, God entered into a new covenant with man, opening to man a new way of access into fellowship with himself. There is strong evidence that not just the early church but Jesus himself thought in these terms and that he was consciously the fulfillment of the promise that was inherent in the whole work of God in the Old Testament.

Fulfillment, however, has both a positive and a negative relation to the past. We can see this most clearly in Jesus' relation with John the Baptist, which we may take as representative of his relation with all the witnesses to God's word in the past. Jesus affirmed his continuity with John when he let himself be baptized by him and spent time in his company before the beginning of his ministry, when he said that none greater than John had lived before him, and when, in answer to those who questioned John's right to do as he did, he implied that his and John's authority were the same in kind. They were children of the same Wisdom. Yet he asserted also his divergence from John and refused firmly to be pressed into the pattern of message and ministry that had been established by John. In short, Jesus' unity with John the Baptist did not commit him to a uniformity with John in word and practice. In the same manner we conceive of the relation between Jesus and Elijah. Jesus' coupling of the names of Elijah and John the Baptist would suggest as much; John was like an Elijah come back to life. The God of Elijah who refused to share the allegiance of Israel with any other god is the God and Father of Jesus who in his gospel of the Kingdom lays claim to the total self of man. Both Elijah and Jesus find the sickness of man in the dividedness of his being. For Elijah it is the worship of Baal and the whole pattern of life that goes with that worship which contradicts and negates the true worship and service of God. For Jesus the issue is more subtle, the suppression of external forms of idolatry having driven idolatry inward, so that God's rivals for man's worship are found in love of possessions, pride in one's own spirituality, devotion to one's own family, loyalty to one's nation, or the reverencing of sacred laws in such a way that the God from whom the laws come is forgotten. But Jesus is as ruthless as Elijah in demanding the worship of God alone and in his recognition that wholeness and health in the life of man are impossible unless he lets himself belong to God in this unconditional fashion.

The solitariness of the prophet is also a point of contact with Jesus. Elijah seems to himself to be standing alone against the world. He is to discover that he is not as alone as he thinks; God still has seven thousand faithful worshipers in Israel; yet he has constantly to wage his battle alone, with no one on whom he can depend for certain support. So also Jesus has to stand alone, his own family alienated from him by their inability to understand him and his closest disciples failing him in the final crisis of his

life. We may ask whether it was this sharing of a common solitariness in the face of overwhelming opposition that made Jesus
feel that Elijah was so close to him in the experience of the
transfiguration. If we need yet another point of unity between
Elijah and Jesus, we might find it in their common concern for
victims of injustice. When a king and queen arrange a murder
in order to get their hands on Naboth's property, Elijah speaks
out for Naboth at risk of his own life. There is no such dramatic
incident in the life of Jesus, but there is a consistent identification of himself with the poor, with the outcasts of the community, with the naked, the hungry, the homeless, the prisoners,
the victims of the callousness not of royalty but of ordinary men
and women in society.

The essential unity of Elijah with Jesus Christ, as servant of
the word of God which in the fullness of time was to be incarnate in Jesus Christ, can then be asserted. But this unity places
no stamp of approval upon all the actions and attitudes of Elijah.
He cannot be made into a model of Christian conduct or a guide
concerning how to conduct the Christian battle against the forces
in the community that are antagonistic to a Christian order. We
are disciples not of Elijah but of Jesus Christ, and Elijah has significance for us only as one whose ministry and witness were
fulfilled and thereby purged of their dross in Jesus Christ. Whatever in the ministry of Elijah, or in the tradition concerning that
ministry as preserved for us in the book of Kings, stands in contradiction to the ministry of Jesus Christ has no authority for
us as Christians. Our relation to Elijah is like our relation to
John the Baptist, an indirect one mediated by Jesus Christ. The
ministry of Elijah or of John, fulfilled and reinterpreted by the
ministry of Jesus Christ, has limited authority for us in determin-
ing our ministries. Elijah and John were men who in protest
against the corruptions of society fled to the wilderness and not
only by their food and dress but by their whole manner of life
commended an ascetic tradition of faith to their fellow countrymen. But Jesus, in witness to the love of God, which seeks man
where he is in human society, invaded the communities of Pales-

tine with his gospel and delighted to eat and drink with men who needed him and his ministry that they might know that the life he offered them took up into it joyfully such common things as bread and wine. We can understand the protest of the asceticism of Elijah and John, and we can understand why through the ages many Christians have been drawn to follow their example in similar situations, but we have to remind ourselves that the ministry we share is the ministry of Jesus Christ, which is not world-denying but world-affirming, and that it brings its most shattering judgment to bear upon human society not by turning its back upon it but by an unconditional openness to it, loving it, bearing the burden of its sins, and bringing to men the consciousness that this concrete everyday world in which we live is none other than God's good creation.

The Miracle of the Fire from Heaven

The next problem with which we must deal is the miracle that forms the climax of the drama enacted on Mt. Carmel, the fire which in response to Elijah's prayer falls from heaven and consumes both the sacrifice and the water in the trough surrounding it. The full miraculous character of what is described is concealed frequently by naturalistic explanations. The most frequent one is that the " fire " was a lightning bolt, which opportunely and providentially flashed to earth at that moment with destructive force. But this is not what the narrator intended. The fire in this instance is identical with the fire which in II Kings, ch. 1, Elijah calls down from heaven to consume two companies of soldiers. A much cruder naturalistic explanation was offered some years ago by a commentator who surmised that it was not water which Elijah poured over the sacrifice but oil from a nearby outflow of oil, thereby turning the whole thing into a gross example of trickery. But the comments of most interpreters evade the problem of the miracle of fire from heaven. Norman Snaith in *The Interpreter's Bible* suggests that it may have been lightning from heaven. F. W. Farrar in *The Expositor's Bible* writes at great length about the impossibility of the miracle of Elijah's being fed morning and evening by ravens when he was in hiding beyond the Jordan and then passes over the fire from heaven as though it were the most natural thing in the world. John Skinner in the *New Century Bible* asserts simply that the reality of the miracle must be assumed because otherwise the whole history of Elijah would be dissolved into legend. Rudolf Kittel is content to say that a historical event must lie at the root of the story, but although he recognizes the problem that such a narrative furnishes for the serious historian, he makes no attempt to reconstruct what actually happened. Ronald S. Wallace, in a recent book, *Elijah and Elisha,* finds the fire from heaven the necessary supernatural manifestation without which the Israelites would not have been converted, and then at once allegorizes the fire for Christians, the fire from heaven for which the modern Christian must pray being the baptism or descent of the Holy Spirit with tongues of fire.

But do we really need to be so restrained and apologetic in dealing with the element of miracle and magic in the stories of Elijah? When we compare the figures of Elijah and Elisha in Kings with the figures of Amos, Hosea, Isaiah, and Jeremiah as they stand before us in the books that bear their names we are immediately aware of legendary accretions that have grown up around the former as traditions concerning their activity were passed down by word of mouth in Israel. The power of an Amos lay solely in his word, and we can surely have no doubt that the power of an Elijah resided primarily also in his word. But with the passage of the years the power of God manifest in the prophet came to be conceived as something more direct and visible than the hidden power of the divine Word in human words. Therefore there was attributed to him a power over nature, to control the rainfall, to divide the waters of a river, and to call down fire from heaven to serve the purposes of his ministry. A false reverence in the approach to these legendary details actually has the effect of concealing where the power of God resided in the prophet Elijah. The story is told by Skinner and Wallace as though all would have been lost in that crisis of Israel's life if God's power had not been made visible to the eyes of the Israelites in the fire that fell from heaven. But is not this a serious underestimation of the power of God's word not only in Elijah but in all the prophets of Israel? Which faith has the greater promise for the future, one that is based on a visible demonstration of divine power or one that is a response of heart and life to the claim that the sovereign God makes upon the human self in his word? Why is it not sufficient for us that Elijah in a crisis of Israel's faith had the boldness to stand out at danger to his own life in protest against the flood of pagan Baalism and to demand of Israel a decisive answer to the question: Who is the living God?

In order to understand how such tremendous powers came to be attributed to prophets, we need to take account of the awesome powers that are validly claimed by all the prophets not for themselves but for the word that they serve. The word of God with which they have to do has in it creative and re-creative power. It formed the worlds and in it is hidden the power to create a new heaven and a new earth. As God's word of judgment, it can bring destruction on men and nations. Before it, kings tremble and bow down, and the poor take courage because, while it brings the mighty low, it lifts up the poor and weak and burdened of the earth. By this word the most monstrous powers of wickedness are overthrown. It has in it life and death according to man's response to it. This is the power residing in the prophet which encourages the growth of popular legends about all manner of miraculous and magical happenings for which he is responsible. In the legends, however, the power that is hidden in the prophet's word is externalized and made visible in outward events. We have to take account of the fact that the mind of man constantly tends to externalize the acts of God. Movements that belong in the realm of the spirit in the relationship between God and man are described as though they were visible events and movements. Moses' vision of God in Ex., ch. 3, is a typical prophetic vision. He sees a fiery presence and hears the voice of God out of the fire, but the tradition externalizes what is seen by Moses and describes it as though it were a happening that anyone who was there might have observed. Paul, to whom

Christ appeared in a similar fashion, in a fiery, blinding light and a voice that sounded out of the light, had his life transformed by this personal confrontation, but if we examine the three accounts of the experience in The Acts, we shall find that the process of externalization was also at work there. In one account the companions are said to have seen the light but to have heard nothing; in another they are said to have heard a voice but to have seen nothing; these contrasting accounts enable us to observe the process of externalization directly at work. The activity of God in the realm of the unseen begins to be reported as though it were an event in the external world visible to the physical eye or audible to the physical ear. In emphasizing the reality of the invisible event, language begins to be used that compromises the character of the event.

What are we to do, then, with this marvelously dramatic story of Elijah's encounter with the prophets of Baal? Are we to read it to our congregations and our pupils and then warn them not to be too impressed with the miracle of the fire or to be led by Elijah's final act of vengeance to think that God expects us to slaughter his enemies? Or shall we lay it aside as likely to do more harm than good? Or shall we frankly face the fact that much of the Scriptures is equally open to misunderstanding so that it must constantly be interpreted in the light of the gospel if it is not to lead people astray? It is not only the Old Testament but also the New Testament which must be brought to the test of the mind of Christ. Scripture has its center in Jesus Christ and must be interpreted from that center if it is to sound in our ears not with a confusion of voices but with all its voices blending into harmony with the one voice that we must hear and obey, the voice of our Lord. Therefore the one question that ultimately concerns us is whether we can hear in this story of Elijah a word that is at one with the Incarnate Word.

BETWEEN GOD AND BAAL

The situation in which Elijah found himself is a timeless one, reproduced in varying forms in every nation in every age. What

Palestinians worshiped as Baal reappears constantly in human life as men seek their self-fulfillment elsewhere than in a God of righteousness and truth. The austerity of the worship of Yahweh sends men in throngs to the shrines of Baal, where they find an easy tolerance of the importunate demands of nature. The priests of Baal understand what men want and give it to them at a price. Nor is it necessary to give up the worship of Yahweh in order to enjoy the pleasures of the cult of Baal. The man who has his head on straight keeps a foot in each camp, in Yahweh's camp for respectability and in Baal's camp for pleasure. And when the king himself becomes a model of double-mindedness, it is only natural for the common man to copy his example. All that is necessary to secure conformity with this deadly order is to silence the voices of all who might be so foolish as to speak out against it. But in Israel in the ninth century B.C. there was one voice that could not be silenced, one prophet who was careless of his own life, and, like both Jeremiah and Jesus, he had to blurt out the truth no matter what men did to him. Elijah knew what his countrymen all seemed to have forgotten: that only in faithfulness to its covenant relation with God had Israel any promise of life, and that unfaithfulness to God would corrupt the heart of the nation and bring it destruction from within. That he had to stand alone did not dissuade Elijah from his protest. One man with God had firmer standing ground than ten thousand men with Baal. He was sure of his cause. And when he issued his call to Israel to choose between God and Baal and challenged the priests of Baal to test their faith against his, he became for all time a voice ringing in the ears of men, calling them to decision and daring them to compare the strength of their idols with the strength of the living God.

Let no man disparage Elijah because so many legends have sprung up around his figure. None of the legends can conceal the integrity of his prophetic vocation or the sharpness with which he cut into the rotten and dangerous situation of his time. Criticisms of the tradition concerning him should not encourage any attitude of condescension toward him as though we had passed beyond him in the things of God. We face situations in our own time comparable to that which he faced in his, and we have to ask how many of us are bound to God as he was bound or have a courage of faith comparable to his in standing against the tide of popular religion, which so often conceals its paganism under a mask of superficial piety. We may not approve the way in which Elijah is said to have planned to demonstrate the power of his God and the futility of the idols, but we dare not come short of him in our willingness to expose our faith and to let its validity be tested in comparison with the false faith of our day, although we may look for God to vindicate the true faith in some less dramatic way than that of sending fire from heaven. And even the fire from heaven has something to say to us. What the ancient narrator was trying to convey with his fire from heaven was a valid truth concerning the God of Israel: that he was a living God. The idols that men worship are dead. They have no power. They can do nothing. They are emptiness and deceit. But the living God of Elijah acts in the midst of his people. He is a fire that burns. He is like rain in the desert, which transforms it into an Eden. He does not sit on a shelf with a nail in his base to hold him firm, and grin foolishly at his worshipers. He comes to them in judgment but also in love, that he may take them into covenant with himself and open to them glorious new possibilities of life.

No! We do not have to set this story aside or apologize for its presence in Holy Scripture. We have just to hear it, but hear it in its true context as part of an Old Testament in which men have heard and responded to the call of God's word but have not yet had fully revealed to them all that is promised to man or all that is claimed of man, a fullness that could not be known until it was made flesh in Jesus Christ.

VI

JEREMIAH AND THE PROBLEM
OF CHURCH AND STATE

IN THE TWENTIETH CENTURY the message of the great prophets of
Israel has seemed to many people to be one part of the Old
Testament that can be made directly relevant to the life of modern man. Churches that had been shaped to a large extent by the
evangelical revivals of the eighteenth and nineteenth centuries
and therefore had their interest focused almost entirely upon the
saving of individual souls experienced a refreshing liberation
from their individualistic concentration when historical scholarship made them acquainted with the comprehensive and searching social concern of the prophets. Here were men seven centuries
before the time of Jesus exercising a ruthless and devastating
critique upon the society of their time, exposing the injustices,
dishonesties, hypocrisies, and general corruption that were poison-
ing the life of their nation, and trying not just to save individual
souls out of the ruin but to persuade their community that the
justice, righteousness, and mercy demanded of them by God were
the only solid foundation on which to build for the future. It was
providential that the rediscovery of the prophets took place in the
nineteenth century as the problems of modern industrialization
became constantly more acute, because it at least kindled here
and there a sense of social and economic responsibility, far too
little, certainly, to affect the general situation appreciably, but at
least a seed that had the possibility of growing in the twentieth
century into a dominant concern of the worldwide church. We
dare not underestimate the extent to which it is still resisted by

a type of piety that would like the church to confine its attention to " purely spiritual " matters and that becomes not only nervous but even angry when the church in the name of God speaks out on issues of economic and political importance. Against this false spiritualizing of the gospel, which is usually linked closely with extremely conservative and reactionary policies in economic and political matters, the prophets provide a powerful antidote, since it is not difficult to demonstrate that their God who was so intimately concerned with what was happening to his people economically and politically is the God and Father of Jesus Christ. Jesus cannot be separated from the prophets of Israel, since he was consciously the fulfillment of the revelation of God's will and purpose that had been unfolding in them. He reaches back into the Old Testament across the intervening centuries of Judaism and establishes a unity between the prophets and himself. Paul tells us that the prophets, together with the apostles, form the foundation of the church, with Jesus Christ at their center as the chief cornerstone binding them into one.

However, when we examine what has been made of the prophets as inspirers of social justice in the modern scene, we detect a number of aberrations in the dialogue with them. Frequently a social ethic has been extracted from their writings but the entire theology in which it was rooted and of which it was a product is left behind. This is parallel with what some distinguished modern moralists have tried to do with the New Testament. They admire the way of life that was inculcated by the Christian gospel and appreciate the great contribution that it has made and makes to civilization, but the theology of the gospel is completely incredible and inadmissible to them, so they seek to detach the ethic from the theology and provide it with a more acceptable modern context. What has been done with the prophets belongs in this context, for a set of social ideals has been extracted from them and made the basis for a program of reform in human society but without much heed being paid either to the rootage of the prophet's social concern in the covenant relation between God and Israel or to the consistent conviction of the prophets that no essential improvement was possible in the social situation until there was a restoration of the integrity of the covenant relation.

WHERE THE PROPHETS BEGIN TO TROUBLE US

We do not understand Jeremiah or any of the prophets until we take account of the theology that underlies their ethical demands. It is basic for them that what man is in his relation with his fellowman and what he is in his relation with God are inextricably intertwined. Man's nature is such that he has the promise of life only in unconditional openness, trust, and obedience toward God. He is himself and realizes his true life only when the very nature of God is reflected in his existence. He lives by hearing and responding to the word of God. But to hear is to know himself the object of God's love and the instrument of his purpose. Truly to hear, therefore, is to be held in a covenant bond with God which at one and the same time lays upon the human partner in the covenant the responsibility to see God's justice, truth, and purity reflected in human relations and liberates him to act justly, to speak the truth, and to resist the corruptions of his environment. Thus the prophets are not to be conceived of as social idealists sponsoring a program of reform. They call for a radical change in the whole order of life in the community, but they have no illusion that the community can or will reform itself. The source of the corruptions is diagnosed by them as a breach in the relation between God and Israel, and until that covenant relation is restored, there is no prospect for the future except death.

Perhaps against this background we can begin to spell out some of the points at which the modern man begins to have difficulty with the prophets, especially with a prophet such as Jeremiah. First, the prophet proceeds on the assumption that the covenant relation into which God calls man in his word and in which he sustains him by his word is the only possibility of life for any man. For Israel as for any Israelite, to become deaf to that word and to seek his life outside the covenant is to embrace death, or at least to take a turning that leads ultimately to death. And by death is meant the actual physical disruption and destruction of the community. Neither the man of Jeremiah's day nor the man of today finds it reasonable that his response to the word of God should be a matter of life or death. The prophet seems to him to exaggerate the importance of his concern. After all, he is only one voice among many voices, and we have to weigh them all. He has a contribution to make to the improvement of society and we hope to benefit from his contribution. He sharpens our eyes to detect the injustices of the social order and communicates to us something of his own passion for justice and truth. But we would feel foolish to make the issue as sharply urgent as he does. Injustice for us is an imperfection of human society, not a rebellion of man against his God; and the way to deal with it is by education, agitation, and the improvement of the laws, not by threatening society with God's judgment and calling men to respond in faith and obedience to the God who confronts them in his word.

That leads to a second point of disagreement. The prophet seems to have entirely too narrow a view of how God is known to men. Here we must distinguish between how God deals with men and how he is known to them. The two are sometimes confused. He deals with them in the concrete events of their history. Essential to the faith of the prophets and expressed in the conception of God as Creator of the world and Lord of history is the conviction that every event in the life of man has a place in the unfolding of God's purpose for him. God is in it. The ultimate meaning of all that happens is hidden in God's purpose. To the outward sense, events are just happenings in a human world, but the eye of faith finds hidden in them the acts of God, acts of judgment and acts of mercy. But how does the eye of faith have power to penetrate to such meanings? Certainly the prophet does not endow the human mind and spirit with such penetration. His answer is that of Amos: that God does nothing without revealing what he is doing in his word. His word reveals his acts. This does not mean that each happening requires a special word to explain it. God's word is primarily the self-revelation of God in his word, his making of himself known to his people. We are enabled to understand the hand that is dealing with us in the events of our lives when the word of God reveals to us the heart and mind behind the hand. But the insistence of the prophet is that no man truly knows God except through this word in which he is revealed in judgment and mercy, never in mercy without judgment and never in judgment without mercy. In contrast to this, modern man congratulates himself that he has much broader access to a knowledge of God. He has only to look into the face of nature or into the depths of his own being to be conscious of God. He has a divine truth of his own that is only deepened and enlarged by the word of God to which Scripture bears witness. He has a truth in his religious tradition that is equally valid alongside all that he hears from the prophets and apostles. The prophet seems intolerably narrow-minded in his reliance on the word of God alone and in his distrust of all else that men take to be revelations of God.

A third point at which a number of the prophets, including Jeremiah, are likely to give offense today is in their attitude to established religious institutions. There is a general attitude of approval for religion and religious institutions in America in our time that very definitely the prophet would not share. His harshest condemnation is usually reserved for representatives of religion who in their zeal to please and to capture the loyalty of people for religion offer ways and means of being on good terms with God that completely misrepresent the covenant relation. For Jeremiah, " judgment begins at the house of God." The perversion of the religious institution poisons the life of the nation at its source, and when that perversion takes place in the interests of a blind and selfish nationalism the institution pronounces its own doom, however outwardly impressive it may appear. Again the prophet is likely to seem fanatically extreme and utterly unbalanced in his judgment. Why is he not content to expose the abuses of religion? Why must he, like Jeremiah — and also like Jesus — announce the coming destruction of the Temple, which has become the center of the perversion of religion?

The Temple Sermon

This long introduction has had the purpose of making us more attentive to the sharp contours of the historical incident that we have before us and to warn us against taking our stand too quickly at the side of Jeremiah in the conflict that he provoked. It has first to appear where we *belong* in the picture. It could be that our present religious attitudes make it impossible for us with honesty to associate ourselves with Jeremiah in his situation.

First, then, let us reconstruct the incident. We are fortunate in having a double report of it, in chs. 7 and 26 of The Book of Jeremiah. In ch. 7 the attention is focused upon Jeremiah's sermon in the Temple court in which he denounced the hypocrisy of a nation that made a great show of religion in the ceremonies of the cult but had little interest in doing what God commanded in the life of everyday, reaching his climax in a prediction that the Temple would shortly be destroyed. In ch. 26 the sermon receives more summary treatment and forms only the prelude to an account of what happened in consequence of Jeremiah's attack upon the Temple: the immediate angry uprising of the crowd led by priests and prophets so that Jeremiah's life was in danger, the attempt to secure his condemnation as a traitor before the princes sitting as judges in the New Gate of the Temple, and the intervention of some of the princes led by Ahikam, the son of Shaphan, which saved the prophet's life. It is significant of the role of the people in the story that in ch. 26:8 they are together with priests and prophets in demanding the death of Jeremiah, whereas in v. 16 they are described as giving their support to the princes who said, " This man does not deserve the sentence of death."

The incident took place " in the beginning of the reign of Jehoiakim the son of Josiah." That would place it in the year 609 b.c. The tragic death of King Josiah a short time before as he attempted to block the northward march of the Egyptian Pharaoh at Megiddo had brought a brief and hopeful era to an end. Earlier in the seventh century the nation had seemed to be rushing to its doom under the depraved and bloody rule of Manasseh. But under Josiah there had been a dramatic revolution.

The prophetic party had gained the upper hand and a timely rediscovery of the Mosaic law had inaugurated a far-reaching religious reform. Shrines throughout the land which had become centers of a paganized cult were suppressed by Josiah, and the worship of the nation was brought under strict control in the Jerusalem Temple, which itself had to be purged of its pagan practices. The religious purification was accompanied by a corresponding political unification. Josiah extended his rule northward into the territory of what had formerly been the Northern Kingdom, Israel, and, as he became more powerful, intense national aspirations began to center upon him. It seemed possible that the fortunes of the nation were about to be restored. The death of Josiah did not end such hopes. After a brief three-month reign of Jehoahaz, the son of Josiah, the Egyptians, who now regarded Judah as a vassal, placed his brother Jehoiakim on the throne in his stead. Jehoiakim had his father's dreams of greatness but neither his principles nor his character. The pagan tendencies, which had been only suppressed under Josiah, were not slow in taking advantage of the new situation. Of course, an orthodox exterior was preserved, the ceremonies of the Temple being conducted with the greatest magnificence and popular enthusiasm, but outside the Temple the order of life was in glaring contradiction to everything that God required of a people in covenant with him.

There is considerable uncertainty concerning the attitude of Jeremiah to the reform movement in the days of Josiah. There is evidence of his esteem for Josiah, and there can be no doubt that he would heartily approve the suppression of the paganized shrines and the purgation of the Jerusalem Temple. But where some scholars find in his early sermons an indication that he participated actively in the movement for reform, others believe that he must have seen from the beginning that the reformers were more interested in a reconstruction of the cult to make it more impressive and powerful than in a cleansing of the daily life of the nation. The one thing that is certain is that, whether early or late, he recognized the superficiality of the reform and struck out vigorously at those who " have healed the wound of my people lightly, saying ' Peace, peace,' when there is no peace " (ch. 6:14). By the time of Jehoiakim he had come to recognize in the " reformed " Temple nothing less than the chief obstacle to true religion. The pagan idols had been torn down, or hidden away out of sight, so that now the nation thought of itself as worshiping God in truth. But actually the Temple and not Yahweh was the object of their confidence and loyalty and had become a new and even more treacherous idolatry than the more obviously pagan practices of earlier times. We can imagine how offensive Jeremiah's attack on the Temple and its worship must have been to the cultic priests and prophets who took a great pride in the religious reform that they had accomplished and who could not understand how anyone who believed in God could be against them. How offensive also it must have been to the people who were under the impression that to speak against the Temple was tantamount to speaking against God!

We do not get to the bottom of the situation, however, nor can we understand the intensity of the passions roused by Jeremiah, until we see the close relation between the religious enthusiasm that was focused upon the Temple and the nationalistic aspirations that were being encouraged by the Temple priests and prophets in cooperation with King Jehoiakim. Jehoiakim thought of himself as a new Solomon. He began to build magnificent palaces with forced labor (ch. 22:13) and to live in the most luxurious style. One prophet named Uriah who opposed him and spoke against what was going on in the Temple was hunted down by him and eventually executed, even though he fled to Egypt for safety. The king understood how valuable to him could be a religious enthusiasm that remained under the control of ecclesiastics who were responsive to his orders. The Temple, therefore, had become a symbol of national confidence and patriotism. The building itself was a magnificent one, having been erected three and a half centuries earlier in the prosperous days of Solomon. It was a reminder to the people of a glorious past that might someday return. Its stones were so massive that it seemed impregnable, and the ritual to which they listened when within it excited their minds with dreams of great things yet to come. To attack the Temple was to attack the nation's heart and to lay oneself open to the accusation of being an enemy of one's own people, in short, a traitor to the national cause. Jeremiah was calling into action against himself the most dangerous force in any land and in any age, the force of blind and fanatical patriotism. So closely intermingled had the interests of religion and nationalism become in Judah that a prophet could not deal with the perversion of religion without laying himself open to a charge of treason.

This incident becomes specially interesting to us as Christians because of the way in which it stands in line with another attack upon the Temple that came over six hundred years later. Like Jeremiah, Jesus accused the priesthood of having profaned the Temple, and he too predicted a day when not one stone would be left standing upon another. But there was no prince such as Ahikam to intercede for him when the death sentence was demanded by the priests to rid the land of such a dangerous agitator. Because Jesus' clash was with Sadducees and priests, sometimes it is not recognized that what he offended was not just religious interests but an intense nationalism that had its emotional focus in the Temple. A very significant interpretation of Judas' betrayal of Jesus is given by a rabbi, Jacob Golub, in a textbook on Jewish history. In Golub's portrayal of the Christian movement, Judas is represented as a patriot who, although a disciple of Jesus, came to recognize how dangerous Jesus was to the whole future of Judaism, and in loyalty to his nation reported what he knew to the authorities. The tragedy of Judas, then, was that of a man in whom loyalty to the nation proved stronger than the faith in God that had been generated in him in his relation with Jesus Christ.

There is a peculiar significance in the fact that priests and prophets desired the death of Jeremiah for what they took to be a treasonable act, while the princes, who were the politicians of that day, took a different view of the matter. Evidently they were not so blinded by nationalistic fervor as were the religious leaders. Some of them who had learned their statesmanship under Josiah were perhaps already distrustful of the rash policies of Jehoiakim and aware of their need for a strong prophetic voice such as Jeremiah's to halt the dangerous trend in Judah's life. But the priests and prophets were completely blinded by their nationalism. Under the illusion that they were defending their God and his Temple, they had become simply the passionate and murderous proponents of a national policy that was already paying them substantial dividends.

THE MODERN PARALLEL

It is not difficult, then, to locate the point at which the Jeremiah of this incident enters into dialogue with modern man. The only churches in the modern world for which nationalism is not a temptation and a snare are those which have to carry on in the face of antagonism and persecution at the hands of the government of their land. We are living in a day of intense nationalisms. Of course, it is much easier to recognize at a distance than close at hand. When it takes the extreme form of German Nazism or Italian Fascism and makes a bold and open confession of its intentions, everyone can see it. But when it is more restrained and polite and professes to be nothing more than the reasonable self-interest of one's nation, it may go quite unrecognized. It is a serious mistake to think that nationalism is no problem until its ambitions impel it to march across the borders of its neighbors. There are as many brands of nationalism as there are countries in the world. If you are an Egyptian, you can recognize Israelite nationalism but you cannot recognize the Egyptian brand. If you are British, you can recognize the French one but not the British. If you are American, you are acutely conscious of Russian and Chinese and Cuban nationalism but not of the American kind. If you are Argentinean, you recognize it in Brazil but not in the Argentine. You see, what in the other country is a dangerous nationalism seems always to be transformed into an admirable patriotism in one's own country.

What makes the problem of nationalism so urgent for the church today is that we happen to live in an era when the power of the state has become inflated until it overshadows all other institutions and makes serious encroachments on the life of every individual. Concentrations of economic and political power in corporations and labor unions within the state require a powerful government to control them. The demand for social services and guarantees makes it necessary for the government to take over by taxes the spending of a large part of the national income. The threat of total war forces upon the government a military budget so large that a high percentage of the population finds itself directly or indirectly working for the government, and at the same time it makes everyone willing to submit to measures of control that formerly would have been accepted only in wartime. Then, the possibility of rapid mass communication by radio and television, added to the use of the press, affords a government the opportunity to control the minds and attitudes of its citizens as never before in history, and psychology has opened up a knowledge of the workings of the human mind which those who wish to control their fellowmen for their own purposes can use in a perfectly devilish way. We have also to contend with a modern demand for efficiency that makes democratic processes seem intolerably wasteful to some eager minds, so that the national interest appears to them to demand a large amount of regimentation. Add to all this the tendency of a nation to transmute the way of life that it has found most advantageous to its own interests into an idealistic creed that becomes sacrosanct and unchallengeable, and top it with the inclination of religious leaders to identify this national creed with the creed of their religious institution, and you have the situation that many Christians have to face today.

The problem as it confronts the church in the United States has its parallels in other countries. The word " nationalism " is likely to suggest some erratic and voluble movement that quickly discredits itself with all intelligent people by the idiocy and impracticability of its proposals, although even in that form it may in some places have made serious inroads upon Christian congregations. But the really dangerous nationalism in each country is not so easily recognized nor so quickly repudiated by intelligent people. Will Herberg in a serious sociological study of the religious situation in the United States, published under the title *Protestant — Catholic — Jew,* claims that very widely in all religious institutions the fundamental loyalty is to the American way of life and not to the traditional creed of the institution. What would he find if he made a similar study of religion in other countries? The church, founded upon Jesus Christ, subtly and imperceptibly shifts its allegiance, so that the interests of the church and of the nation become identical, and it is taken for granted that there can be no serious or radical tension between the two. To such a church Jeremiah stands as a warning, first that if it intends seriously to maintain the tradition of the prophets and of Jesus Christ it must expect to have some uncomfortable words to speak to the nation from time to time, and second, that when it makes itself little more than the religious representation of the national interest, it has made itself unworthy of a future in the eyes of God.

SEPARATION OF CHURCH AND STATE?

It has sometimes been thought that this whole problem can be avoided by a policy of absolute separation between church and state. The illusion is then created that only where there is a state church, as certainly was the order in Judah in the time of Jeremiah, does the problem become difficult, and that free and independent churches are in no peril from this quarter. But each of us is born with the problem concealed within us, for we enter upon life as members both of our nation and of the church of God. We cannot deny either of the two loyalties. Sooner or later we have to face the question of which of them is to have precedence over the other. The idea that a neat division can be made between the two areas of interest fails to take account, on the one hand, of God's claim to sovereignty over the whole of life and, on the other hand, of the constantly expanding claim of the modern state to regulate the lives of its citizens. If the church would moderate God's claim and limit its concern to the so-called " spiritual life of man," keeping its hands off all such unspiritual matters as politics, economics, and the problems of society in general, there would be no difficulty. But we have learned to be suspicious of anyone who wants the church to be " purely spiritual " and to confine its attention to the souls of men, because invariably his concern is not for the spirituality of the church but only for his own freedom to do as he likes in social, economic, and political matters without having to hear any restraining or rebuking word from the church. What is at stake here is nothing less than the sovereignty of God in his creation and the integrity of the church as his spokesman in the midst of human society.

It begins to be clear, then, that Jeremiah's Temple sermon sounds with peculiar sharpness into our modern scene and confronts us with difficult decisions. If faithfulness to God's word demanded of Jeremiah such intransigent resistance to the popular religious and political enthusiasms of his time even at risk of his life, what does an equal faithfulness to God's word demand of us in our modern situations, which have in them so many parallels to that of Jeremiah?

We too live in a time of religious reform. The past fifty years have seen tremendous changes in the life of most Protestant churches. There has been theological reform. Early in the century there seemed to be only two alternatives, an optimistic, doctrinally vague but social-minded religious liberalism and a narrowly literalistic, severely dogmatic but earnestly evangelical conservatism. But the recovery by the church of its roots in a Biblical and Reformation theology has liberated it from this impasse and opened up new possibilities of development. There has been institutional reform, largely through the influence of the ecumenical movement, which has brought individual Protestant denominations out of their isolation and made them open themselves to fruitful relationships within the one great church of Jesus Christ. There has been educational reform, old mechanical and slipshod methods giving way to thorough and much more intelligent approaches to the educational problem. There has been liturgical reform, as churches have learned to utilize the store of devotional experience and wisdom that comes to them out of the past and to ask themselves how worship can be most meaningful today, instead of merely following an established pattern woodenly. There has been reform also in the church's approach to the world, not just in new missionary situations but also in old established communities. But just because we have lived through these and other reforms, in every instance reforms which in fifty years are only begun, we are in danger of a new complacency, of being satisfied with changes that have grazed no more than the surface of the problem and have left the actual existence of the community unmoved. All reforms in the life of the church are endangered by the outward appearance of initial success. We need to know, as Jeremiah did, that it is easier to change the external practices of a people and of their institutions than their day-by-day existence. But, most important, all reforms are in danger of being taken to be " the " reform in the life of church and community that God desires, the healing of the " wound of my people," the restoration of the covenant bond in which a people is once more wholly at God's disposal. Until this ultimate reform begins, nothing essential has been changed, no matter how far-reaching the changes on the surface of life.

What is likely to shock the modern reader, however, is not Jeremiah's criticism of inadequate reforms but what must have seemed to the people of his time to be an attack upon a venerable religious institution. It was quite right for him to criticize the Temple and its functionaries, but he went too far when he predicted its destruction. But perhaps we have much greater respect for religion and religious institutions than God has. Many scholars are deeply troubled by the reports in the New Testament that Jesus denounced the religion of the Pharisees, because they have discovered that the typical Pharisee was deeply in earnest about moral standards and the maintenance of a pure worship of God. It is hard for us to think that any religion in which men are in earnest about their belief and practice can be other than a good thing. But neither Jeremiah nor Jesus shares with us this indiscriminate approval of religion. On the contrary, they were made keenly aware in the crises of their ministries that religious earnestness is no guarantee to a man that he stands with God. Much of the most passionate resistance of man to the will of God is offered in loyalty to religion and religious institutions. A man's religion may be his strongest line of defense against God's actual claim upon him. This does not mean that we declare war on religion in the name of God. We cannot escape from religion or from involvement and participation in religious institutions. But we can be awakened to the peril of religion, that both in its personal and its institutional form it can in its very earnestness become an idolatry, openness and trust toward the living God being replaced by trust in our own religiousness or religion. It is here that we have to be brought into a narrow pass by the absolutely unique revelation of the Scriptures, for where else than here do we hear a word from God that brings even our most passionate religious devotion under a searching judgment?

Nowhere is the peril of religion more obvious than when religion and patriotism become intermingled and hopelessly confused the one with the other. Does this mean, then, that the Christian must suppress his patriotism in order to maintain his unconditional allegiance to God? There have been Christian groups which have thought they could preserve the purity of their faith only by refusing to participate in such public responsibilities as voting or holding public office or serving in the Armed Forces. But withdrawal is not the answer. Loving God with all his heart and soul ought not to make a man love his country less or more restrainedly. On the contrary, to love God is to love our neighbor and to serve our neighbor. Jeremiah was not less a patriot because of his faithfulness as a prophet. On every page of his writings one can feel the depths of his love for his nation, and it was both love for God and love for his nation that made him risk his life over and over in the effort to turn Judah aside from a course that he recognized must lead quickly to ruin. Resistance to a blind nationalism is at one and the same time an act of faith and an act of true patriotism. Nationalism in all its forms is a dangerous idolatry, a setting of the nation and the national interest in the place that belongs only to God, and the church that fails to give warning of the peril of such idolatry is disloyal not only to God but also to the nation of which it is a part. A church that fails to stand with Jeremiah will find no neutral position that it can adopt but will be forced relentlessly to stand on the other side with the priests and prophets who found Jeremiah so deeply offensive.

VII

SECOND ISAIAH AND THE
PROBLEM OF THE FUTURE

THE THEME of the 1954 Assembly of the World Council of Churches in Evanston, Illinois, was " The Christian Hope," calling for an investigation of what the Christian faith has to say concerning man's future. The widespread reaction of many North and South Americans was one of incredulity: that churchmen should be brought from all around the world simply to discuss eschatology! With so many important subjects of immediate and urgent practical concern available, why would anyone light upon such a remote and impractical theme? But European Christians felt very different about the matter. To them this was a most practical and urgent theme. The whole future not only of the church but of humanity seemed to them to hinge on the recovery of an understanding of the sources of a really Christian hope in relation to the future. Eschatology for them was no peripheral matter but central and vital for man's survival.

Here we have an excellent example of how what we hear in Scripture is influenced by the whole context of life in which we do our listening. The future is not consciously a problem to most Americans, both North and South Americans, because they subscribe to a " success " or " progress " motif in almost every area of life. The nation, as it has moved from one frontier to another, has seemed to have limitless possibilities of growth and development before it. Every institution within it, not only businesses but schools and churches, thinks constantly in terms of expansion. So also the individual charts his career, whether he be clerk, scientist, lawyer, educator, or minister, with confidence that there is an open door into the future and that the degree of his success will depend almost wholly upon his own efforts. Man makes his own future, and what he makes of it comes from his handling of the present, not from any Christian speculation about the future. It is this secular confidence concerning the future which makes so many Christians uninterested in eschatology. They do not expect their future from God, either as individuals or as a society. Such an expectation would seem to them irresponsible. Rather, they respond heartily to the appeal of the valedictorian who calls his classmates to go forth boldly into the world and shape a better future for man. Therefore they turn a deaf ear to those portions of Scripture in which man is encouraged to expect great things *from God* in time to come.

The European who has seen two world wars devastate his continent and the ugly sores of Nazism and Fascism break out at various points in his proud civilization has had his confidence shaken in man's ability to shape a future in which his children will want to live. He has tasted despair. His artists draw sketches of " man without hope." For him there is no inevitability about human progress. Modern educated man has shown a remarkable ability to walk backward at the very time when he was most certain that he was going forward, and to do the things which make war inevitable while with his conscious mind he was seemingly working most earnestly for peace. Science which was to transform the world into an Eden has presented him with the atomic bomb, and it is hard for him to be encouraged by the thought of its beneficent constructive uses as long as missiles lie concealed on either side of him poised at his cities and able in a few moments to wipe out all that a thousand years has constructed so carefully. The future is problematic. There is no longer any reasonable human basis for believing in the possibility of a future. And it is when the events of life have driven men into the depths of such despair that they are given ears to hear and value the theme of hope in Scripture.

Is there a hope that remains when from a human standpoint

the situation has become utterly hopeless? At this point the insistence of Scripture that it is the nature of God to create a future where to the human eye there is no possibility of a future becomes good news, to be listened to with care, to be received with thankfulness, and to be tested with courage as one tests the ice of a river to see if it will bear his weight and carry him across to the other side. Biblical eschatology has an interest only for men who at last have discovered that no future worth having can be of their own making and who have become willing not only to hear what the Scriptures have to tell them about their future but also to receive their future, both as individuals and as a society, and above all, as a church, from God.

MEMORY AND HOPE

Basic to our consideration is the fact that human beings are so constituted that they require both memory and hope in order to function in the present. We may have the illusion at times that we are living wholly in the present, but we can make nothing of our present experiences until they are interpreted in the context of what we remember from the past, and we cannot bear the weight of the present moment unless we have the hope that something else will be possible in the future. Memory and hope are like two wings without which man cannot even stand upright, much less fly. Take away from a man every vestige of hope for the future and you have paralyzed him, perhaps destroyed him. Viktor Frankl in the story of his experiences in a German concentration camp tells how men who lost all hope lay down and died. Man cannot live and breathe without a future. But neither can he make sense of life without a past. A man who has lost his memory can no longer perform the simplest functions for himself. The experiences that form the background and basis for all judgments and actions are no longer available to him. But what is true for individuals is equally true for societies. History and eschatology are the two wings of the present. History is the memory of the past that alone makes present experience meaningful and intelligent action possible, and eschatology is the vision of the future that gives direction to the present and confidence to take the next necessary step toward a future goal. Perhaps now we begin to understand why there is so much history and eschatology in the Bible. They belong together. God's purpose for us compasses the whole of our life in time, past, present, and future. We never live simply by what he is to us now. We have continually to look backward to what he has been to us and forward to what we expect him to be to us in time to come in order to sustain our faith in him in the midst of the darkness and uncertainty of the present.

A Prophet of Hope

We turn now to a prophet who continually looked to the past and to the future in order to survive in the present. No other prophet appeals to history so explicitly as does Second Isaiah. Remember, remember, remember, he counsels Israel. "Have you not known? Have you not heard? Has it not been told you from the beginning? . . . The everlasting God . . . does not faint or grow weary." "Look to the rock from which you were hewn, and to the quarry from which you were digged. Look to Abraham your father." Remember how God called a world into being in creation, he says, and know that he can call a new world into being now. Remember how he delivered you out of the land of Egypt when there seemed to be no future for you and gave you a great future in a new land, and know that the same kind of deliverance is possible now. All this remembering of the past, all this looking back, is for the purpose of preparing the eyes of faith to look forward and to see through the darkness of the present into the future that God has made ready for his people.

The eschatology of Second Isaiah, like that of the earliest Christians, was completely unreasonable. There is evidence that some of his fellow countrymen found his hopes ridiculous and mocked at them, just as the contemporaries of the first Christians must have thought them half-crazed to be expecting the imminent return of their Master to carry his cause to universal victory. Moreover, what embarrasses present-day Christians about Biblical eschatology is that the critics both of the prophet and of the early Christians seem to have been proved right by history. Jesus Christ did not return on the clouds of heaven to bring history to an end. And in the sixth century B.C. there was no sudden dawning of a new age in which the righteous were vindicated and their oppressors exposed and punished. If that were not sufficient to make modern man distrustful of Biblical eschatology, then there would also be the sad history of Christians who at various times have renewed the intense Biblical expectation and have waited breathlessly for the great day of judgment and vindication to burst forth. Some have even sold all their possessions and gathered on a hill in their neighborhood to await the moment. But always they have been disappointed and have had to turn back to take up the commonplace tasks of life again. Or perhaps we have known Christians for whom eschatology is a kind of sacred game in which they take various statements about the future which they find in Scripture, particularly in the books of Daniel and Revelation, and piece them together in order to disclose to a credulous audience what is going to happen next in world history. They make of the Bible a crystal ball into which you have only to gaze in the right way and you will be able to know the things that are going to happen before they happen. Such misinterpretations and misuses of Biblical eschatology as these have been responsible for many Christians' giving it a wide berth and have frequently seemed to ministers to be valid reasons for remaining silent on the whole subject.

We cannot rightly grasp how unreasonable Second Isaiah's hopes for the future were until we know the situation of his people in the sixth century B.C. and the promises he addressed to them in the name of God. Second Isaiah seems to have lived about the middle of the sixth century, close enough to the disasters at the beginning of the century which had shattered his nation to remember them vividly and yet far enough from them to feel that Israel had already been punished twice over for all its sins. He spoke to a people scattered in many lands, north, south, east, and west. There had been Israelites in Assyria ever since the deportations of the late eighth century; they had been there for nearly two hundred years. There were Judeans in Babylonia, a distinguished population of nobles, priests, prophets, and leading citizens who had been carried away in 597 and 587 B.C. But many had fled from the stricken land to other countries. One contingent had gone to Egypt, taking the prophet Jeremiah along with them in spite of his contention that they should remain in Judah. Syria and other neighboring lands would receive their quotas of refugees.

By far the majority of the population, however, remained in Palestine. Frequently even in histories of Israel this last point has not been adequately recognized. It takes more than the heavy hand of a conqueror and the devastation of cities and towns to drive farmers off their land. Cities take years to rebuild, but the land will produce a fresh harvest the next summer. The farmer may have to live in a cave in the rocks, and the lack of strong defensive towns may leave him exposed to the marauding exploits of rapacious neighbors, but he will survive. And even in the ruins of Jerusalem life will go on. There will be priests to offer sacrifices on the altar amid the ruins of the temple. There will be businesses springing up out of the wreckage to carry on the trade of the community, and soon some will have more than they need while others are starving and homeless (Isa., ch. 58). There will be a form of government and law courts. There will be religious fast days and other observances directed by the priests. But beneath the surface there will also be a continuation of pagan practices that a generation earlier made both Jeremiah and Ezekiel certain that Jerusalem could not escape the destroying judgment of God. This seems to have been the kind of community that confronted Second Isaiah in Palestine. It has always been difficult to fix his location with definiteness because of the fact that in most of chs. 40 to 55 he is addressing a people scattered in many lands, but, if the unity of chs. 56 to 66 with chs. 40 to 55 is recognized, we begin to find evidence in both sections of the book of just such an immediate community in Palestine as I have described. Sometimes the prophet speaks to the people who are close at hand. At other times he speaks past them to the whole nation in its dispersion. But in whatever direction he turns he looks out upon a people that is perishing in its despair about the future.

Thirty-five or forty years is a long time for a broken nation to wait for healing to come. The Book of Jeremiah shows us that some Judeans interpreted their disasters as evidence of the weakness of Yahweh and transferred their worship to the universally popular Queen of Heaven. There would be others who would deduce from the successes of the Babylonian armies the superiority of the Babylonian gods and would begin to look to them for help. Second Isaiah's repeated attacks on the folly of idol worship in which he fairly scorches the idolaters with his ridicule indicate to us the serious inroads that idolatry had made on the life of the nation. But even those who resisted idolatry and held fast to their faith in Yahweh must have grown weary with waiting for mercy to follow judgment long before thirty-five years were past. These people were the special concern of the prophet, for undoubtedly he had been one of them himself, with "weak hands . . . feeble knees . . . [and] a fearful heart" (ch. 35:3-4). The "weary" (ch. 50:4) who walk "in darkness" and have "no light" (v. 10) and who cry out in their despair, "My way is hid from the Lord, and my right is disregarded by my God" (ch. 40:27), have not yet abandoned their faith, but they are so burdened and obstructed in it that it is unlikely to survive long unless some light shines into their darkness. The earlier prophets had convinced them that the sufferings and misfortunes of their nation were the judgment of God upon its sins, but as the time of judgment continued year after year it began to seem to them that what they were experiencing was not a purifying judgment, but rather, an outright rejection. Yahweh had abandoned them. The covenant relation would never be renewed. Their sins would never be forgiven. Jerusalem was like a desolate and impoverished wife whom her husband had divorced (ch. 50:1).

Into this situation like the blast of a trumpet sounded the message of Second Isaiah: God has forgiven Israel! The decision has been made in heaven, and soon the effects of it will be seen on earth. The time of judgment is past and a great new day for God's people is about to dawn. The covenant relation between Yahweh and Israel which alone has in it the promise of life is to be restored. All of this is expressed in powerful dramatic form as God's return to Jerusalem. Already he is on his way. The voice of a herald can be heard calling for a great highway to be made ready through the desert and across the mountains. Note that the text says "a highway *for our God*"! God himself is about to appear in majesty and glory to show before the eyes of all men that Israel has been forgiven and remains still the people of his purpose. Jerusalem is told to get up to the top of a high mountain and proclaim to the cities of Judah that God is at hand. No longer are they to be sheep scattered helplessly across the face of the earth. Yahweh, their shepherd and their king, is with them once more to gather them and to guide them.

The full eschatological force of the language of ch. 40 has frequently been concealed by interpreters' failing to see that it is God's forgiveness and God's return to his people on which the prophet's attention is focused. We have been told that what he really was saying, in a rather high-flown poetic way, was only that shortly the Persian king, Cyrus, would release the Jews in Babylonia from exile so that some of them would return to Palestine and a great new day for the nation would begin. But there is not the slightest indication of this anywhere in the chapter. The great good news is much more daring and not based in any way upon the observation of what an earthly ruler might do. God is about to act in such a way as to confound all earthly rulers and to show that in comparison with his power their power is as nothing. Second Isaiah was not announcing anything so diminutive as the mere return of a few hundred exiles from Babylon. If we look forward into the succeeding chapters, we shall see that he was announcing a new era in the life and history of Israel, a transformation of poor, weak, trampled Israel, broken and discouraged, into a great and powerful nation that would rule for God over the whole earth. Twice he says that it is to be nothing less than a new heaven and a new earth. The kings and queens of the nations are to carry the exiles home from all the lands in which they have been scattered, not just from Babylon, but from the four corners of the earth, and out of the nations are to come multitudes who will join themselves to Israel, recognizing that in this people alone is the one true God known and worshiped.

What basis had Second Isaiah for such a hope as this? He tells us in vs. 6-8 of ch. 40 and in many other passages in his writings. God's word to Israel in the past revealed his purpose for his creation and for mankind. Israel was chosen to be the bearer of that word and the human instrument for the fulfillment of that purpose. Kings and empires may rise and pass away; all that is human may be like the grass of the field that is green today and tomorrow is gone; but the word of God is imperishable. The glory of Israel in the past was its experience of the absolute faithfulness of God to his word. Whatever he promised came eventually to fulfillment in history. Even the bitter years of Israel's punishment were witness to the faithfulness of God, for he had promised Israel life in the keeping of the covenant but death in the breaking of it. The God of Israel holds the world and man in the hollow of his hand. The future will be determined not by the might of Babylon or Egypt but by the will and purpose of God, already hidden in the heart of Israel in the word that has been received from God. That word is like rain or snow that falls from heaven on the deserts of human life with power to transform them from a wilderness into an Eden (ch. 55:10-11). Therefore those who put all their trust in the word in which God's nature and purpose are revealed and who are willing to wait in confident expectation for what God is yet to do will be able to walk with firm step through the darkness of the present, rejoicing in anticipation of the victory that is certain to come. Such will be the strength that is born of hope.

This may sound very impressive for the moment, but we have to meet the objection that none of the things that Second Isaiah said were about to happen ever actually happened. He hoped for a rebirth of his nation and an ingathering of the scattered citizens to Palestine so that the land would overflow with them, but all that happened was that a generation later a few came back from Babylon, and the city of Jerusalem continued defenseless and impoverished for more than another century. He hoped for the triumph of Israel over all its enemies, but they were to remain a subject nation for centuries to Persians, Greeks, Syrians, and Romans. He hoped for a marvelous fruitfulness for Palestine, but it remained the same rocky, grudging soil that it had always been. He hoped for an Israel purified and enlightened that would be the teacher of the nations, guiding them into the ways of righteousness, but Israel was to become more and more concerned with itself and less and less interested in being a light to the darkened world. He hoped for God himself to come and by his power create a new heaven and a new earth, but the old heaven and the old earth refused to pass away. Are we then to dismiss his eschatology as merely a somewhat unfortunate expression of prophetic zeal and to look for the modern significance of his message at some other point? If we do, we shall remain blind to the very heart and wellspring of the prophet's joyful faith and unconquerable hope and shall condemn ourselves to a superficial understanding not only of what God meant to him but also of what God can mean to us.

THE ESSENCE OF ESCHATOLOGY

The greatest mistake one can make is to imagine that eschatology has to do only with the expectation of certain events in the future. The primary expectation is not of this or that, of fabulous enrichment for the nation or victory over the forces of evil, but simply of the vindication of God's purpose in history. In short, all the different, concrete expressions of hope are really attempting to say that the day will come when the beauty and glory and joy of the fulfillment of God's intention for his creation will be visible to all mankind. In the darkness of the present moment the facts of life seem to contradict God's sovereignty. The will of man seems able to resist and even to overcome the will of God.

No one can believe in God's sovereignty in his creation unless his ear has been opened by God's word to the mystery of what God is doing in history. God's hand is hidden now. It is always hidden in the outward events, so that he cannot be known directly, for to know him directly would be to know him without faith and without decision. But there have been those to whom he has disclosed what he is doing and by that disclosure has taken them into his purpose and made them the servants of his design for mankind. To them the past is the history of the unfolding of that design, and since God cannot be unfaithful to his own nature and purpose, the future must be the completion of what he has begun. Eschatology, whatever form it takes, is therefore the expression of a profound and unshakable confidence in the sovereignty of God in his creation and in history which in honest recognition of the contradictory phenomena of life finds that sovereignty always hidden in mystery at the present moment. The concrete forms in which this confidence is expressed are secondary, so that a delay in the coming of the expected day, the failure of God to appear and vindicate his servant, or the experiencing of humiliation instead of victory, far from destroying the hope, seems only to make it more intense. After all, what matters is that God will vindicate his sovereignty, whether tomorrow or ten thousand years from now, which means that God is sovereign now in spite of all that seems to contradict it. Where such a faith and hope as this persist, men are able to go singing through the darkness, and no situation however hopeless it may seem to be is able to take from them the assurance that God has a future for them in which the destiny that he designed for them will be fulfilled.

But there is more to the prophet's eschatology than this. It represents a conviction that man's life in time is going somewhere. Events do not just follow one another in meaningless procession; they move steadily toward a goal. Even the disasters and misfortunes of life receive their meaning in the light of the goal. What God is to man at the beginning of the way gives him a vision of the goal and is understood by him as a promise in the strength of which he can dare to move out boldly into the un-known. He moves out, seeking the fulfillment of the promise, looking earnestly for " the city which has foundations." This is the faith that gives birth to history and to the writing of history. The Greeks had no such idea of history as movement in time toward a meaningful goal. For them, history moved in circles, ever coming back to where it began and repeating itself. History with meaning and purpose was born in Israel, the product of an eschatological faith, and, perhaps, where that faith vanishes history must inevitably become meaningless and purposeless, an endless turning in futile circles. Abandoning the Biblical escha-tology, man in the modern age, that is, in the last two centuries, has substituted for it a secular hope, a belief in human progress based upon his own reason and his genius in mastering the forces of nature. Christians unconsciously make this substitution, noting only that the Biblical hope has ceased to interest them and not recognizing that something much more serious has happened — that their faith in God no longer has anything to do with their future, that their future is to be of their own making and not in any way God's gift to them.

ESCHATOLOGY AND ETHICS

One aspect of Biblical eschatology which is not often recog-nized but which is to be seen clearly in the ministry of Second Isaiah is its consequence for ethics. Critics of eschatology have frequently interpreted it as a fixing of the eyes upon a distant future to the neglect of the ethical responsibilities of the present. But no such criticism can be leveled at Second Isaiah. It was his grasp of God's intention for Israel that made him an irrecon-cilable rebel against everything in the existing order that resisted or contradicted that intention. It was his vision of a world in which all men would find their perfect freedom and fulfillment in worship and obedience toward God that made him intolerant of any narrow and limited definition of Israel's destiny. He con-stantly measured the world he knew against the new world that was yet to come and refused to let his countrymen make any compromise between the two. Waiting upon God meant an unconditional openness to the word of God, which the prophet called " trembling at my word " — a word that called men to feed the hungry, clothe the naked, shelter the homeless, and see justice done between man and man in the life of the community.

There is both an urgency and a patience in this kind of waiting. It is not a waiting with folded hands, but rather, with outstretched hands, outstretched toward God and God's future. Those who wait for the Kingdom are hastening toward the Kingdom with eagerness, impatient for its establishment in every department of life. They are hungering and thirsting for God's " righteousness," which in Second Isaiah is a synonym for God's great new era. Yet this impatience is not inconsistent with a profound patience, a patience that is willing that God should do all things in his own time and is able to bear the incompleteness of now because of the certain hope of what is yet to be. Biblical eschatology is the death of all utopianism because for it the full unfolding of God's purpose requires the whole of time from the beginning to the end. Man in time is ever on his way toward the goal. There are no devices by which he can force God's hand and shorten the journey. Therefore both the knowledge of God and the fulfillment of God's purpose in any one moment are broken and sadly incomplete. To expect God to be fully revealed now so that there is no darkness or uncertainty, to expect an order of life to be established now in which perfect justice will prevail, or to expect a church now in which there is no ignorance or uncharitableness or indifference is to forget that it is to take the whole of time for God to bring humanity to its promised goal.

God's Coming

Finally, we have to understand why in Scripture men of faith are constantly looking for God's coming. This is unfamiliar to us in our customary ways of thinking. We are more likely to dwell on God's existence rather than on his movement or action. He is the One who *is* rather than the One who *comes*. In fact, we are puzzled that a God who is omnipresent should be spoken of as coming. We need to be aware then that this is a use of earthly language to describe an unearthly event. Scripture also speaks of a "coming" in the human self that is not intended to denote an external movement but rather a movement of the human spirit in an intangible dimension ("Come unto me," Matt. 11:28; "The Spirit and the Bride say, 'Come,'" Rev. 22:17). The opening verses of Isa., ch. 40, make very clear that God's "coming" to Jerusalem is meant to describe the restoration of the intimate covenant relation with his people. God can be spoken of as forgiving or as coming, and both denote the same event. But God's coming is meaningless unless it is meaningful to speak of his absence, just as forgiveness is meaningless unless men have known what it is to stand under the deep shadow and in the agony of God's judgment. For that reason we delude ourselves when we assure ourselves too lightly of God's presence and take for granted that he is with us. An honest confession would acknowledge God's absence, the vacancy in us and in our world where God is not, or at least not yet. That which holds man on the brink of an abyss is the hollow at the center of his existence, even at the center of his most religious existence, into which God has not yet come. In the very moment that he rejoices at signs of the coming of the Kingdom, he has to be aware of this hollowness and pray passionately, "Thy kingdom come." Prophets, apostles, and above all, Jesus Christ, knew the world as it is in the eyes of God and therefore knew how broad and deep is its resistance to God's sovereignty, so that never in all time can there be a moment when it is not waiting for the coming of its King in judgment and in mercy.

VIII

THE TWO ISRAELS

WHENEVER WE READ Isa., ch. 53, we have to be reminded that it is still the Old Testament that confronts us. The words are so eminently fitted to describe the sufferings and death of Jesus Christ and have been used so often to do it that his figure rises up before our eyes and fills the whole horizon. " He was despised and rejected by men; a man of sorrows, and acquainted with grief." " Surely he has borne our griefs and carried our sorrows." " He was wounded for our transgressions." " He was oppressed, and he was afflicted, yet he opened not his mouth." " He was cut off out of the land of the living, stricken for the transgression of my people." How can a Christian hear those words and not think of Jesus upon his cross? That is the amazing thing about this chapter: it was written nearly six centuries before the death of Jesus, and yet you would think that someone whose very existence had been torn up and set down in a new direction by that death was confessing his faith. That should be a warning to anyone who is inclined to make a sharp separation between the Old Testament and the New that to say where the one ends and the other begins is not so easy as it first appears. There are other passages in the writings of Second Isaiah, not to speak of other parts of the Old Testament, where we seem to be breathing the very air of the New Testament. But here the shadow of the crucifixion falls across the chapter, reminding us that there was a cross in the midst of the life of Israel pointing forward to the cross of Christ.

But we shall do the Old Testament a great injustice and deprive ourselves of a full hearing of its message if we do not let Isa., ch. 53, remain in the Old Testament and in the sixth century B.C to speak to us out of its own original historical situation. There is a tendency in some quarters today to think that a Christological interpretation of such passages as this demands of us the assertion that it was written directly about the Messiah. Let it be granted that the whole of Scripture has its center in Jesus Christ, reaching forward to him for centuries and then reaching forward *from* him, and granted too that wherever God's word makes itself heard it is the word that in the fullness of time was to be incarnate in Jesus Christ. The word of God is one because it is God in his word, and there is but one God, the God and Father of Jesus Christ. Therefore we do right to hear the voice of our Lord in the words of the First Commandment, "Thou shalt have no other gods before me." And we do right to see the face of our Lord when the words are said or sung, "He was despised." Yet we dare not let this be made an excuse for laying a coating of New Testament meanings over the text of the Old Testament, a practice that is likely to make us careless about getting at the original meaning of the text or unable any longer to see with clarity into the original historical situation. First we must do our historical work with diligence to permit the text to speak in its own century; then we may expand the Biblical context to find what light is thrown upon the text from the center of revelation in Jesus Christ. But if we neglect either of these steps, we shall undoubtedly miss something of importance that the chapter has to say to us.

One of the greatest mistakes that can be made in regard to Isa., ch. 53, is to isolate it from its context. The uniqueness of its content has long tempted scholars in this direction. In the last decade of the nineteenth century Bernhard Duhm with his unfortunate theory of the "Servant Songs" detached this chapter, together with three other passages, from the main body of Second Isaiah's writings, and other scholars, observing the contrast between the highly individual figure of the servant in ch. 53 and the collective figure in chs. 42 and 49, isolated it still further. But there are indelible marks upon the chapter that link it with its context, and there are aspects of the prophet's way of thinking and writing evident in the chapter, recognition of which is essential to the understanding of the chapter. It will be sufficient to deal with four of these.

First is the highly dramatic style in which the prophet expresses himself, so distinctive and so different from the style of any other prophet that it should be sufficient to identify any writing of Second Isaiah's. He speaks with many voices. Sometimes it is as though God himself were speaking directly; at other times the prophet speaks in his own person. Again, Israel as the servant of God speaks, but on other occasions an Israel that is in rebellion against God lets its voice be heard. There are changes also in the direction of the speaking: God may address Israel, or he may address the nations of the world. As a consequence one has constantly to ask who is speaking and who is being addressed. Chapter 40 begins with God calling for someone to take word of his forgiveness to Israel. Then voices are heard, one heralding the approach of God as he appears in glory, another commanding the prophet to preach the good news of God's approach. At v. 12 a sudden change takes place as the prophet attacks sharply the blindness of those who think the nations too strong for God. Chapter 42 furnishes an even more striking example of these dramatic shifts. It opens with God addressing the world in general concerning his servant Israel who is to establish a just order in the earth, but in v. 5 it becomes an address to Israel assuring the nation that it is to be a light to the nations. In vs. 10-12 the whole earth is called to sing for joy at such a prospect. In v. 13 the prophet describes God going forth like a man of war to carry out his purpose, but in vs. 14-17 God himself tells what he is about to do. In vs. 18-20 God ponders sadly the deafness and blindness of his servant Israel, but in vs. 21-25 it is the prophet who does the pondering concerning the sad plight of his people and their inability to lay to heart the meaning of God's fiery judgment under which they have languished so long. We must be prepared, then, for sudden changes and for an imaginative and dramatic form of presentation.

With this background we approach the opening verses of ch. 53. We ask ourselves who is speaking and to whom. We recognize that we are listening to a confession of sin and blindness by someone who until a certain moment had paid no heed whatsoever to the servant of God's word. He speaks for himself and for others who were familiar with the pitiful figure of the servant, yet wholly unimpressed by him. To them he was a poor weak creature, unlikely to say or do anything significant, not only unattractive but positively repulsive. They interpreted his misfortunes and sufferings in an orthodox fashion as God's punishment of his sins. The confessor does not admit any personal responsibility for the servant's sufferings and death. Someone else seems to have had that responsibility. He admits only that he and his kind went their way in utter indifference to what was happening to the servant. But now all is changed. In some way the blindness has been struck from his eyes and he has made the astonishing and humbling discovery that God's mighty intervention for the salvation of his people was in none other than this despised and broken figure. " Who would have believed that which we have heard! " The suffering of the servant was not for his own sins but for the sins of his blind and heedless brothers. He went to his death that he might strike the blindness from their eyes and lay them open to the forgiveness and healing of God. From v. 7 on, as the death of the servant is described and beyond his death a victory is promised him, there is a subtle shift of speaker at several points. While the voice interprets the suffering as " the will of the Lord," it is as though the voice of God broke through without interrupting the flow of the sentences or of the thought: " stricken for the transgression of *my* people " (v. 8), and then in vs. 11-12 it takes over completely in order to announce the impending victory and vindication of the servant. Thus we see how the prophet speaks from behind various masks.

A second factor of which we become aware in the prophet's writings in general is the intense eschatological expectation in which he lived and which made him so uniquely the prophet of hope in the Old Testament. The full force of his eschatology has been obscured by the mistaken notion that his hopes were roused first by what seemed to him the possibility of a new era being inaugurated by the Persian king, Cyrus, and that when he exulted in the approach of a new dawn for Israel he was really expecting no more than that Cyrus would permit the exiles in Babylon to return to Palestine and begin life afresh. Second Isaiah's eschatology has its closest parallel in the eschatology of the early Christian community. There is no sign in it of any sober weighing of historical possibilities. On the contrary, it anticipates a fantastic transformation of the human situation. There is to be not just a tiny dribble of returning exiles from Babylon, released by Cyrus, but an ingathering of Israelites from the four corners of the earth, carried home by those who have been their masters and bringing with them the riches of the nations. But the great day of redemption is to see far more than Israelites in Palestine. The true God is to be acknowledged by many from among the nations, and they are to join themselves to Israel, swelling its ranks and making it a mighty nation. The rocky soil of Palestine is to know a marvelous fruitfulness, and the desert places are to become productive gardens. But what matters most is that from Jerusalem a light of truth and justice is to shine out to the ends of the earth, Israel becoming a nation of priests and ministers through whom witness is borne to the reality of their God. Since some of the earth's inhabitants may be expected to resist God's order, Israel is also to be the instrument of God's judgment for the overthrow of every force of evil.

The detailed description of these hopes for the future may easily create the wrong impression, as though the prophet kept up his spirits in a difficult time by concocting dreams of a future that was never to materialize. When we penetrate to the core of his faith, however, we find there a simple confidence that since God, the God of Israel, is sovereign in his own creation, the purpose for the world and humanity that he has revealed in his word in Israel must ultimately come to its consummation. God's word cannot fail. God's purpose cannot be defeated. The first fruit of this confidence is courage and strength to go steadily forward in the present darkness when the forces that resist God's purpose seem to have the upper hand and the prospect for the future is grim. If God is sovereign in his creation, then he is sovereign now, and those who trust themselves to him can endure even the bitterest persecution without losing heart. The future will be determined by God and not by his enemies. The spelling out of the shape of that future is a secondary matter. It may take fantastic and contradictory forms, but these are only exuberant expressions of the confidence that God's sovereignty, which is obscured in the present, will be openly vindicated in the future.

The intensity of this eschatological hope appears vividly in ch. 50 where the servant, experiencing painful insults and hateful persecution, sets his face like flint to endure whatever men may do to him, since " he who vindicates me is near." At any moment the great change may come when God will show his hand openly to the humiliation of the wicked and the joy of those who tremble at his word. The same intense hope creates the atmosphere of ch. 53. The hour has been one of darkness. The servant has gone to his death, refusing to defend himself before his unjust accusers. The curse of God has seemed to rest upon him. But these are only outward appearances. To the eye of faith the hour has been one of victory. God's arm was laid bare in the death of the servant. Strangely, in him and in his sufferings and death in faithfulness to God's word, God struck a mighty blow for the overthrow of his enemies. There is a greater victory yet to come when the servant will see, and all men will see, what God has been doing in this strange way. But already in the darkness God has shown himself sovereign by using the death of his servant to break through the blindness and indifference of men and win them to himself.

A third clarification that is provided by the context is the identity of the servant. No other problem in the whole of the Old Testament has had so many suggestions offered for its solution. For centuries it was taken for granted by Christians that the servant in Isa., ch. 53, is the Messiah, and modern scholars as eminent as C. C. Torrey and H. H. Rowley have supported this interpretation. Other scholars, convinced that in ch. 53 the servant is a single person and not a dramatic personification, have searched through the history of Israel for an individual who would fit the character. A dozen names have been proposed, the most frequent one being that of the prophet himself, in spite of the unlikelihood that he would describe his own death and attribute such profound consequences to it. But when we consult the writings of Second Isaiah as a whole and recognize the inseparableness of ch. 53 from them, there is no longer any mystery about the identity of the servant. Israel from the beginning of its life has been the servant of God's word, marked out to be the instrument of God's purpose in history by that word being hidden within it. But not all of Israel has ever accepted that destiny. Also, from the beginning of its life Israel has been a rebel and a sinner against God, and still in the prophet's day, in spite of God's fiery judgments, remains obstinately deaf and blind to his purpose. In every generation there have been two Israels, Israel according to God's intention and Israel the rebel against God's intention. It is impossible therefore to identify the suffering servant of ch. 53 with Israel as a whole, as though all the sufferings of the centuries that the nation had endured had a redemptive significance. The prophet makes very clear again and again that many of his people's misfortunes have been the just consequence of their sins. The suffering referred to in ch. 53 is not just any suffering; it is suffering in faithfulness to God, suffering at the hands of one's fellowmen, accepted as the cost of bearing faithful witness to God. Who then is the servant? The prophet concentrates into a single portrait the experiences of all who in past, present, and future give themselves to that task. Abraham, Elijah, Jeremiah, and a host of others are included. But there are also servants in the present who remain faithful in the face of scorn and persecution, as we shall see in a moment, a group who are described by Second Isaiah as "those who tremble at

God's word." Perhaps also his mind reached forward into the future to take in those who in time to come would hear and respond to the call to be servants.

The fourth factor in the context that throws light on ch. 53 is the series of references to conflict in the community where the prophet ministered and the evidence that in this conflict the people who stood with the prophet were harshly treated. In ch. 51:7, people who cherish God's law in their hearts and are addressed as "you who know righteousness" have to endure the reproach and revilings of men. The same conflict is reflected in ch. 50:10-11, where those who fear the Lord and obey the voice of his servant are contrasted with others who engage in pagan practices. In ch. 54:14-15, the promise is made to the faithful that soon the time of terror, oppression, and strife will be past. In ch. 57:1, the righteous are described as perishing without anyone paying any heed, and in v. 4 their neighbors who are guilty of pagan practices mock them and make sport of them. In ch. 58:4, certain people who delight in religious formalities such as fasting but are indifferent to the plight of their hungry, naked, and homeless brothers are said to "fast only to to quarrel and to fight and to hit with wicked fist"; in short, the enforcement of the fast day is made an excuse for violence. In ch. 59:6-7, this violence is said to have led to the shedding of innocent blood, and in vs. 14-15a, an anarchic condition is described in which the man who refuses to do evil becomes a prey at the hands of his fellow citizens. In ch. 65 the true servants of God are assigned a different destiny from their paganizing brothers, and finally, in ch. 66 where the prophet condemns those who think they can win God's favor by building him a temple and offering him sacrifices, those who tremble at God's word are described as being mocked and cast out by their brothers.

Surely all these scattered references to mockery, persecution, smiting with the fist, and death itself being inflicted upon those who are consciously the servants of God's word cannot be unrelated to the portrait of the suffering servant in chs. 50 and 53. This does not mean that we should identify the servant at once with the faithful followers of the prophet who evidently paid a high price for their faithfulness. The figure of the servant, as we have already seen, reaches far beyond any one age and comprehends the total destiny of Israel in time as the instrument of God's purpose. But the figure of the servant most certainly includes the little band of faithful believers who were maintaining their witness in spite of all that the community could do to them. Perhaps now we understand the vividness with which the sufferings of the servant are portrayed in chs. 50 and 53. The prophet is not just remembering what prophets and others endured in the distant past in the fulfillment of their task; he draws the portrait of the servant from life, making each line true to what he has seen in his own immediate experience.

If this reconstruction of the historical situation is valid, we can imagine what drew forth from the prophet this tremendous dramatic portrayal of the servant of God in his humiliation and triumph. He was the prophetic leader and therefore the pastor of the faithful believers who walked in darkness in such an evil time. His pastoral concern and warm compassion comes frequently to expression. The sufferings inflicted upon his followers by their community would constitute a serious problem for their faith. Suffering was commonly interpreted as a punishment for sin and a sign of God's anger. Why were they called upon to bear such misfortunes and agony not as a consequence of sin but as a direct consequence of their faithfulness to God? What was God doing that sinners should defy him with impunity and send true believers helplessly to their death? Chapter 53 was the prophet's answer to the agonizing questions of his followers: the humiliation and death of God's servant is to the eye of faith the one and only way to victory. Dying in faithfulness to God, the servant becomes the means whereby God overcomes the blindness of men, humbles them, and heals them of their crippling sin. The death of the faithful is therefore no senseless waste and no sign of God's weakness, but on the contrary, the very point at which God strikes his mightiest blow for the overthrow of evil and the triumph of his saving purpose.

THE TWO ISRAELS TODAY

It is unfortunate that so much of the attention in the interpretation of Isa., ch. 53, has been concentrated upon attempting to identify the figure of the servant. Is it the Messiah? Is it Israel? Is it the prophet himself? Is it King Jehoiakim? Is it Jeremiah? Is it Abraham? But never do we hear any commentator asking the question: Is it I? And yet the whole import of this tremendous chapter is lost upon us until we begin to grasp our own personal involvement in what is set before us here. In fact, we are involved not only in the figure of the servant but also in those anonymous confessors who were blind to God and to what God was doing in his servant.

This chapter speaks to us because we too are a chosen people, a royal priesthood, called to be the light of the world, bearing the promise of healing and salvation to the nations. It is not any superiority that is discoverable in us that has marked us out but simply that our ears have been opened to hear the word in which God speaks comfort to his people. That is our call. That is what constitutes our destiny. God's mighty word of grace and pardon that brings a dead world to life and makes the desert blossom and be fruitful has been spoken to us, and we have received it as one must always receive it, not for ourselves alone but also for our brothers whose life is still being lived in a desert that knows no blossoming. God's word to us is Jesus Christ, crucified and risen, the Light of the World, but to hear and receive that word from God is to be made servants of the word in the midst of our fellowmen, not just believers in Jesus as the Servant of the word but ourselves servants with him in this unique destiny.

There is considerable discussion among scholars as to whether or not Jesus definitely identified himself with the figure of the suffering servant. Certainly there are many passages in the gospels that echo the teachings of Second Isaiah, some of them in traditions that seem to belong to the earliest period. There is good reason to believe that Jesus made use of the concept of servant in the explication of the nature of his mission. But not only does he nowhere explicitly claim to be the servant, but rather, wherever this concept occurs, it seems to be applied to both Jesus and his disciples. In the Sermon on the Mount the disciples are called to fulfill the destiny of the servant and to be " the light of the world," and not until John's reinterpretation of the gospel is Jesus himself called " the light of the world." The mission that in Luke 4:18 ff. and Matt. 11:4 ff. is set forth as the fulfillment of Isa. 61:1 ff. is at one and the same time the mission of Jesus and also of his disciples. When Jesus describes himself as a servant among men he at once calls his disciples to share his servanthood with him. So also in John, ch. 13, when Jesus had performed the menial task of a slave in the company of the disciples, he told them that he had given them an example that they might be servants one to another. Finally, when Paul in Phil. 2:5 ff. portrays Jesus in the form of a servant, his intention is to make clear to his readers that they are committed by their faith in Jesus Christ to share with him the servant destiny. Could it be more clearly or more consistently set before us that to be a Christian is to enter into that great fellowship which spans the ages, at whose center stands Jesus Christ, around whose center stand the prophets and the apostles, but which constitutes a mighty army marching across the centuries and bearing its witness in every generation: the countless servants of God. In The Book of Isaiah this army is Israel, and in the New Testament and beyond it is called the church, the New Israel of God. Therefore if in any degree we know what it is to belong within the church, if we have accepted our share in the mission of Jesus Christ, we are bound to ask what Isa., ch. 53, tells us about our destiny as servants of the word.

Isa., ch. 53, then, is first of all a warning to us how costly it may be to let one's ear be opened to God's word of grace and pardon. In a day such as this when in our eagerness to draw people into the church we are inclined to emphasize the benefits and advantages of a Christian profession, we need to give more attention to such warnings. If we heeded the cross that hangs over the church, we would make it much clearer to prospective members that to enter into fellowship with Jesus Christ is to become servants together with him of the Word of God, with the possibility always of having to suffer and die with him in that service. It was true in 600 B.C. and it is still true in A.D. 1960. The same God confronts the same world, and the same word of God sounds in the ears of men who fight back when they hear from God a word that contradicts their established ways of thinking and acting. The suffering may be evaded by compromising with the world and with the established order, by tempering the sharpness of the prophetic word so that it loses its offense, by working out for ourselves a system of religious words and practices that fits more comfortably into the situation of our times. That is what only too often the church has done, and in so doing it has missed its destiny. It has found a more comfortable and reasonable religious word somewhere outside the Scriptures, and under the impression that it was merely augmenting the divine word of the gospel, it has actually substituted this other word for the prickly, offensive word of Scripture. Here we have at least a suggestion of why the church is bound in such an exclusive fashion to the word of God in Scripture. It is not because the words of Scripture are divine infallible words in contrast to all human words. They too are human words, but human words that bear witness uniquely to the word of God in which God acts for our salvation, in which God comes to man to cleanse him from his sin and to redeem him out of death into life. Where else do we hear that word which at one and the same time is the hope of our future and God's judgment upon all that we are, and where else do men hear the call to become servants of that word no matter what may be the cost?

This chapter also says to us that just as the word of God is hidden from men until it is received in faith as the word through which God enters into covenant fellowship with men and men with God, so also the servants of God are hidden from the world so that God's presence and power in them can be known only to faith. The world can say, " There we recognize a good man," or, " There we recognize a sincerely religious man," but, when the world is confronted with a man who is unconditionally under the sovereignty of God's word and who therefore fails to conform to the accepted patterns of goodness and religiousness in his society, it is puzzled, then contemptuous, and finally intolerant. There is much talk today about the renewal of the church — renewal through liturgical reform, renewal through massive reorganization, renewal through theological discussion, renewal through a return to expository preaching, renewal through study, prayer, and action in small groups. I would not in any way depreciate the importance of any of these endeavors. But are any of them likely to bring significant renewal as long as we remain in the grip of the modern idea that as a church we must be externally and visibly successful? Let us confess frankly that we cannot bear the thought of our church being like a spindly plant growing up out of the dry ground, despised and rejected by men. Unofficially, if not officially, we demand of our ministers that they be successful, or perhaps it would be more nearly correct to say that they demand it of themselves. It is much more damning to be externally unsuccessful than to be merely unfaithful in one's preaching and pastoral duties. In fact, a considerable degree of unfaithfulness will be overlooked as long as the record in terms of membership, finances, and community acceptability indicates success. How can Christian churches so misunderstand what God expects of the servant of his word? There is no hint in Scripture that God expects any speedy external success. Jesus' ministries in Galilee and Jerusalem must both be marked down as failures so far as numbers and acceptability are concerned. Jeremiah failed in everything he attempted. Paul died under the impression that the church as a whole had rejected his gospel. Let us read this passage, Isa., ch. 53, to our people over and over until the truth penetrates their minds and hearts that God does not ask his servant to be successful but only to be unconditionally faithful to the word by which he lives.

Were that all that we hear in Isa., ch. 53, it would be a somber word to the church, somber but healthfully sobering: that God can bring his cause to victory among men only where those who have learned to live by his word are willing to hold fast in their faithfulness no matter what may be the cost. But what transforms it from a somber into a joyous and exultant word is its proclamation that God *is* bringing his cause to victory through his suffering servant. It may be puzzling at first that in our chapter the servant goes to his death and then beyond his death is given his victory. There is no suggestion here of a victory in another world. The victory is on earth. The fruit of his travail which the servant sees is the multiplication of his offspring, the making of many righteous, the coming of the day when not only the lost of Israel but also the blind and the prisoners from among the nations find their way into the freedom of the true Israel of God. It is a mistake and gives a wrong impression to speak of " the suffering servant in Isa., ch. 53." It should be " the suffering and triumphant servant." The suffering and the death are swallowed up in God's victory. This is the vision which enables us to be faithful even when the way is difficult and dark. The road of the faithful servant down into humiliation and death is the one and only road on which there is the certain assurance of triumph at the end of the day.

Undoubtedly we would like to stop at this point, having identified ourselves and our church with the servant Israel. But have we forgotten that there is another Israel in Isa., ch. 53, an Israel which was zealously religious, which loved to offer sacrifices and to hold fast days, which was eager to build a house for God, but which with all these characteristics had no eyes to see what God was doing and no heart to recognize God's word when it was spoken plainly in its hearing? This is the Israel which the prophet elsewhere describes as a sinner and a rebel from its birth. Are there really two Israels, the one the servant of the word and the other a sinner and a rebel, clearly distinguished from each other all through history? Or is there just one Israel with this contradiction buried deep within it, called to be the servant of God's word and in some measure responding, yet at the same time rebelling against the claims that this service makes upon it and constantly seeking a less demanding destiny for itself? If the continuity of the church with Israel enables us to interpret the problem of Israel in the light of the problem of the church as we observe it in ourselves, then we must say that the latter represents the truth. There is just one Israel, but it is ever an Israel divided within itself, again and again having to confess its blindness to what God is doing, its deafness to what God is saying, and its unfaithfulness as the instrument of his purpose. There never comes a time when the confession of the first six verses of the chapter ceases to be our confession. But if it is truly our confession and we have truly been healed and restored by what the Servant of God has borne for our sakes, then we have been bonded into one with that Servant and have come out of our lost state into our true destiny. What meets us in this chapter, then, is what should be meeting us constantly in the life of the church: the transformation of a false and faithless Israel into an Israel with eyes and ears open toward God and man, with tongue unloosed to bear witness and sing God's praise, and with its whole being at God's service to be the instrument of his gracious purpose for all mankind.

Perhaps now finally we see the difference between the fulfillment of Isa., ch. 53, in Jesus Christ, and its fulfillment in us. In identifying the servant not only with Jesus but also with ourselves as the Israel of God we do not make ourselves his equals or in any way detract from the uniqueness of his office. In his servanthood there is no contradiction, for in him there is no blindness and no resistance to the word of God. But the service that his church offers to God has ever been and ever remains a broken service, just as its vision remains a darkened and halting vision. The church is able therefore to have its servanthood, or ministry, only by the mercy of God, only in dependence upon Jesus Christ, that is, only as it ever afresh confesses its blindness and disobedience and is transformed by him from a rebel Israel into a true and faithful Israel. This distinction is lost from sight in some distinguished writings on the New Testament today. The " Christ event " is described as comprehending both Jesus and his church. It has even been said that the term " Christ " includes both Jesus and his disciples. It would be unfortunate if this way of thinking were encouraged by the impression that Isa., ch. 53, is fulfilled both in Jesus and in his church. It is fulfilled differently by the two, and the distinction is of the essence of the matter. In Jesus Christ, God's word found a human servant who by the perfectness of his obedience was the ultimate revelation of God's mind and heart to man and the decisive action of God for man's salvation. But in the church, as in Israel, God's word finds human servants whose most perfect obedience has in it some seed of rebellion and whose clearest vision is always troubled by some persistent blindness. Moreover, this brokenness of the church brings the Israel of the Old Testament very close to us and makes the story of its pilgrimage and the confessions in which it poured out its soul before God indispensable to us as a church as we grope our way toward a more perfect servanthood.

CONCLUSION

Each of our passages of Scripture is witness to a dialogue between God and man; man has his life in this dialogue alone. The various authors are not describing private, inner, mystical experiences that have come to them as individuals but are, each in his own way, pointing to this dialogue as the underlying reality of all existence, whether men are conscious of it or not. Each brings out some aspect of the relation between God and man, but naturally he does it in language and thought forms that were most meaningful to the people of his day. We are able to hear him in spite of our vastly different world and the radical changes in our ways of thinking and speaking only because through all the changes God's dealings with mankind remain the same. The word in which God offers himself to man as the unfailing source of life and understanding and joy and at the same time claims from him an absolutely undivided love and devotion is no different in the twentieth century A.D. from what it was in the tenth century B.C. The God who spoke then still speaks now. Revelation is not something that took place in ancient Palestine and fell silent with the death of the apostle Paul, so that from then on it was only to be remembered. God has no less love for modern man than he had for Israel, and in love he knocks constantly upon every man's door, willing to come in to him and be to him the light of life. It is this consistency of God in his grace and truth which makes it possible for us to read and understand the Scriptures. The words of the text withhold their meaning until the God to whom they witness is recognized as the God who is nearer to us than life and breath in the present moment. This is what Paul means when he says that the Lord who is the Spirit must take away our blindness if we are to read the Old Testament aright. The Lord, the Spirit, is this same God with us now.

What we are saying is that no one can understand the text of the Old Testament merely by reading the words. This holds true for even the most accomplished scholar. He may have at his command the most comprehensive philological, literary, historical, and archaeological information and yet fail to know what the text is really about. The decisive element in interpretation is beyond the scope of his technical equipment. He can master many things but he cannot master the Spirit of the living God. Rather, he has to come under the mastery of the Spirit as did the prophets and apostles, in order to decipher the meaning of their witness. In short, only where men have come awake to the dependence of their lives upon a relationship with God in which God speaks and man responds and have recognized the continuity of that modern dialogue with the dialogue laid bare in the Scriptures have they the *sine qua non* of interpretation. Yet this awakening is itself a response to the hearing of the word of God to which the Scriptures are the indispensable witness.

There may seem to be a vicious circle here: the Scriptures being opaque to our understanding until we are awake to our dependence upon God now, and that awakening being defined as a response to the essential message of the Scriptures. The impasse is one in which we constantly find ourselves and in which we would remain paralyzed were it not that alongside the Scriptures there is a people of God in whose words and life the message of the Scriptures confronts us in flesh and blood with immediacy. The church must be defined not in institutional terms but as a community of faith in which Jesus Christ, the living Word of God, is constantly moving through the world to take away men's sin and blindness and awaken them to God. It is *his* Spirit which is the ultimate interpreter of Scripture.

A further word should perhaps be said about this Christological approach to the Old Testament. There is a widespread fear on the part of Old Testament scholars that it may lead to a disruptive manipulation of Old Testament texts in order to exhibit New Testament meanings in them. And indeed there have in recent years been proponents of a Christological interpretation who have provided a substantial basis for such fears by finding references to Christ in all manner of surprising places in the Old Testament. What is essential, however, is the recognition that the unceasing dialogue of God with man in Israel, to which every part of the Old Testament in some way bears witness, reached its climactic and decisive moment in Jesus Christ, and that the unity of that dialogue is such that not only is the climax robbed of its meaning when the prelude is cut away but the Israelite prelude is never rightly understood until it is seen in the light of how it eventuated. At some points in these expositions the Christological context has appeared more obviously than in others, but it has always been present. It becomes unhealthy if we begin to feel ourselves under obligation in every passage to find a clearly evident line of connection with the New Testament. What matters is that we recognize our unity with the Israel of the Old Testament to be not one that we have devised for ourselves, intellectually or sentimentally, but rather, one that is wholly dependent upon the continuity of the New Israel with the Old Israel consummated in Jesus Christ and in its consummation radically transformed by him. We dare not forget that where the Old Israel becomes the New Israel there stands a cross reminding us that there is discontinuity as well as continuity, a rejection as well as an affirmation. The church forgets that cross at the peril of losing its own distinctive nature.

It may be of help to some who are encouraged to join me in experimenting with the type of exposition that is attempted here if I describe briefly an approach that I have tried a number of times with my students in Union Seminary and which might be used with groups in a local church. It is calculated to make the student sharply conscious of the realities of his present situation in which he must hear and respond to Scripture. I began not in the usual way by establishing the historical setting of the passage but by having the class set down on paper the questions that the passage would be likely to raise in the minds of any careful, intelligent modern readers, whether teen-agers or adults. Anything that would puzzle the mind or would stand in contradiction to the mind of our day was carefully noted. The class was constantly surprised by how many questions appeared, sometimes as many as twenty in a single chapter, and shocked to realize that 90 percent of the questions were commonly brushed over or ignored in the preaching and teaching of the churches. They began to see that a church which ignores the honest questions and difficulties that its people find in the text of Scripture cannot expect them to read it with understanding or to attain any measure of competence either in their grasp of its message or in their ability to interpret its message to others.

Having assembled the questions, we set them to one side for the moment and undertook the historical orientation of the passage. In some instances this was more extensive than in others. We then returned to the questions and considered them one by one in the light of the historical orientation. Frequently we found that in the course of clearing away a difficulty it was as though a door were suddenly opening into the text. We then proceeded to state the overall theme of the passage. What was the primary focus of the author's thought? This proved invariably more difficult than appeared likely at first. It was like finding the queen bee in a hive of bees, because every passage had in it a number of secondary themes that clamored for attention. A common source of misinterpretation of Scripture lies in the making of a secondary theme primary. The whole passage is then thrown off center. But once the primary theme is grasped, the unity of the passage becomes evident and the secondary themes take their proper place in relation to what is primary and to each other. The spelling out of these secondary themes becomes then the explication of the theological content of the passage.

This may seem to be as far as an exposition needs to go, and in fact it is as far as most expositions are accustomed to go. But the theological content is a word of God to us that meets us in the midst of the dilemmas and ambiguities of our existence and demands of us a response. It is a word to which our life as it is, the life of our church as it is, and the life of our world as it is responds in many respects with a decisive " No! " Therefore the final stage of the process with the class was to set down what we called by the rather ugly title, the " anti-themes." We asked ourselves at what points the life of our times contradicts the word that is addressed to us in Scripture or proceeds on a basis completely different from that which is suggested by the passage. The value of this last stage may be illustrated from the remark of one student that he had never before realized that, while on Sundays, and religiously, he thought of the world as God's creation, during six days a week and when he was not consciously engaged in religious thinking he operated with a purely naturalistic conception of the world. Only when this last step is taken do the hidden contradictions that negate the power of the gospel among Christians begin to come to light. Our affirmations of what we take to be Christian truth have little power in them until we bring clearly into consciousness what we must deny if we are honestly to make these affirmations. We never really hear what God is saying in these ancient records until his voice becomes a sword cutting its way through the very marrow of our modern life and forcing upon us choices which we would gladly evade but in which not only our own future but the very future of humanity is at stake.